DISCARDED
Richmond Public Library

D0952060

Bloom's
GUIDES

Tim O'Brien's
The Things
They Carried

1984
The Adventures of Huckleberry Finn
All the Pretty Horses
Beloved
Brave New World
The Chosen
The Crucible
Cry, the Beloved Country
Death of a Salesman
The Grapes of Wrath
Great Expectations
Hamlet
The Handmaid's Tale
The House on Mango Street
I Know Why the Caged Bird Sings
The Iliad
Lord of the Flies
Macbeth
Maggie: A Girl of the Streets
The Member of the Wedding
Pride and Prejudice
Ragtime
Romeo and Juliet
The Scarlet Letter
Snow Falling on Cedars
A Streetcar Named Desire
The Things They Carried
To Kill a Mockingbird

Bloom's
GUIDES

Tim O'Brien's
The Things
They Carried

Edited & with an Introduction
by Harold Bloom

CHELSEA HOUSE
P U B L I S H E R S
A Haights Cross Communications Company
Philadelphia

© 2005 by Chelsea House Publishers, a subsidiary of Haights Cross Communications.

A Haights Cross Communications▲Company

www.chelseahouse.com

Introduction © 2005 by Harold Bloom.

All rights reserved. No part of this publication may be reproduced or transmitted in any form or by any means without the written permission of the publisher.

Printed and bound in the United States of America.

First Printing
1 3 5 7 9 8 6 4 2

Library of Congress Cataloging-in-Publication Data

Tim O'Brien's The things they carried / [edited by] Harold Bloom.
     p. cm. — (Bloom's guides)
   Includes bibliographial references.
   ISBN 0-7910-8171-0 (alk. paper)
   1. O'Brien, Tim, 1946- Things they carried. 2. Vietnamese Conflict, 1961-1975—Literature and the conflict. I. Bloom, Harold. II. Series.
   PS3565.B75T56 2004
   813'.54—dc22
                                    2004014608

Contributing editor: Gabriel Welsch
Cover design by Takeshi Takahashi
Layout by EJB Publishing Services

Every effort has been made to trace the owners of copyrighted material and secure copyright permission. Articles appearing in this volume generally appear much as they did in their original publication with little to no editorial changes. Those interested in locating the original source will find bibliographic information in the bibliography and acknowledgments sections of this volume.

Contents

31143007320618
813.54 Tim
Bloom, Harold (EDT)
Tim O'Brien's The things
they carried

 Introduction

HAROLD BLOOM

Rereading *The Things They Carried* (1990) has prompted me to reread also O'Brien's *Going After Cacciato* (1978). Initially I had read both at their time of publication and remember being more impressed by the earlier narrative. *The Things They Carried* came out of the era of "metafiction": the work of John Barth, Robert Coover, and others writing under the influence of the Argentine fabulist, Jorge Luis Borges, and the "magic realism" of Latin American fiction of "The Boom." Today, *Going After Cacciato* still seems to me a more adequate book than *The Things They Carried*, whose artful formlessness is arch rather than aesthetically gratifying. O'Brien's four books since essentially are repetitions, not so much variants on a theme but fainter echoes of our now faded national trauma, the Vietnam war syndrome.

Now, in 2004, we are engaged in a different quagmire, Iraq, and doubtless we will suffer another trauma. I *want* to admire O'Brien's books more than I do, but they show all the stigmata of Period Pieces, which time will go on rubbing down, until the narratives vanish. Hemingway was always O'Brien's burden of literary anxiety. The narrative voice invariably is that of Nick Adams, itself indebted to Joseph Conrad's Marlow rather than to Mark Twain's Huck Finn, as Hemingway asserted. Perhaps by way of Francis Ford Coppola's *Apocalypse Now*, O'Brien also is dominated by *Heart of Darkness* as well as by Hemingway's *In Our Time*. This is reflected most dubiously by "Sweetheart of the Song Tra Bong," a wholly improbable tale of the metamorphosis of a seventeen-year-old American girl, Mary Anne, into a Green Beret killer. O'Brien is totally haunted by Marlon Brando's countercultural Kurtz, and asks us to accept the tall tale of an Ohio high school girl who ends up as a blank-eyed ambusher, wearing a necklace of human tongues. As a metaphor for

American debasement in Viet Nam, this is too extravagant to be even minimally persuasive. It prompts me to murmur Dr. Samuel Johnson's observation that only just representations of general nature can endure.

Biographical Sketch

O'Brien's true history is this: born in Worthington, Minnesota, the self-proclaimed "turkey capital of the world," in 1946, Tim O'Brien came of age as Vietnam and the Civil Rights movement dominated American culture. He joined the anti-war movement at Macalaster College, described by the *Atlantic Monthly* as "a hotbed of prototypical sixties liberalism." In 1968, he even joined the Eugene McCarthy campaign. But, despite his alliance with counterculture forces, he still went to Vietnam. The feelings described in "On the Rainy River" mirror O'Brien the writer's feelings about his ultimate decision to go to Vietnam. Many critics have suggested that the experience there gave him his voice; O'Brien himself is reluctant to admit the same. At times, he even fights it. In a 2002 interview, Josh Carp said, "You don't view yourself as a Vietnam writer?" To which, O'Brien replied, "In a way I do and in a way I don't. It's like asking Toni Morrison, 'Do you view yourself as a black writer?' Sure, she's had a black experience and her characters are black people, but she'd look at you and have a little frown. And I'm sure Conrad would too if you said, 'You're a "sea writer,"' or Shakespeare if you called him a 'king writer.' ... So on one level, yeah, every book I've written has the shadow of Vietnam on it, sometimes directly and sometimes obliquely." He has also said, "I use Vietnam as a way to get at the human heart and the pressure exerted on it."

He earned a Purple Heart while on his combat tour in Vietnam and, when he returned, resumed his antiwar activities. He also went to graduate school, pursuing but never completing a doctoral degree in political science at the Harvard School of Government. For a short time, he also wrote for the *Washington Post* on international affairs. But by 1973, his writing career took off with the publication of *If I Die in a Combat Zone*, and he has lived as a writer ever since, augmenting his income with intermittent teaching posts at writing colonies and conferences such as Breadloaf. Unlike many of the writers of his generation, he did not hold an academic position until recently. He is now a professor, holding an endowed chair at Southwest Texas State University, where he teaches creative writing.

The Story Behind the Story

Taking its place alongside such work as Michael Herr's *Dispatches*, Le Ly Hayslip's *When Heaven and Earth Changed Places*, Robert Olen Butler's *Good Scent from a Strange Mountain*, Bobbie Ann Mason's *In Country*, and his own novel, *Going After Cacciato*, Tim O'Brien's *The Things They Carried* was both an instant smash and a long-haul classic of Vietnam War Era literature. *The Things They Carried* plays ambitious and wrenching games with truth, understanding, hurt, and more, adding dimension to discussions of postmodernism, literary form, the emerging controversies over creative nonfiction and the work of memoir, as well as larger cultural questions of what constituted "true" experience in war.

O'Brien relished all of it. In interview after interview, he refused to comment definitively on the truth of his work or the truth of his experience except to say that the book was entirely fiction. In the most widely read interview, with D.J.R. Bruckner in the *New York Times*, he stated most plainly that every aspect of the novel was invented: "Tim ... comes originally from Minnesota and is 43 years old. Everything else, even the most convincing personal details about his life and family, is made up." The use of the same name in the narrator was, according to O'Brien, little more than audacious technique. In a 1991 interview for the literary magazine *Artful Dodge*, O'Brien said, in an answer typical of his responses to press at the time:

Hearing a story, being seduced, then having the seducer say, 'by the way, I don't love you, it all isn't true.' And then doing it again. And then saying, 'that also isn't true, just kidding,' and doing it again. It's not just a game, though. It's not what that 'Good Form' chapter is about. It's form. The whole book is about fiction, about why we do fiction ... I'm trying to write about the way in which fiction takes place. I'm like a seducer, yet beneath all the acts of seduction there's a kind of love going on, a kind of trust you're trying to establish with the reader, saying, 'here's who I am, here's why I'm doing what I'm doing. And in fact I do truly love you, I'm not just tricking you, I'm letting you in on my game, letting you in on who I am, what I am, and why I am doing what I'm doing.' All these lies are the surface of something. I have to lie to you and explain why I am lying to you, why I'm making these things up, in order to get you to know me and to know fiction, to know what art is about.

By the time *The Things They Carried* was published, O'Brien had already made a name for himself as a stylist and an important writer and witness to the Vietnam War. His 1973 memoir, *If I Die in a Combat Zone, Box Me Up and Ship Me Home,* and the novel, *The Nuclear Age,* put him on the map, and *Going After Cacciato* had won the National Book Award in 1979. Nearly half of the pieces in *The Things They Carried* had appeared in literary magazines, mainly *Esquire,* and had attracted him much attention. Because of the narrator's name, the presence of an actual memoir in his writing history, and his established penchant for games in his work (*Going After Cacciato* is considered by some to be a good example of American magical realism), interview questions on the work's veracity were inevitable.

As one can intuit from the above, he does not have a daughter named Kathleen. He did marry in 1973, but he had not, before the publication of *The Things They Carried,* ever returned to Vietnam. He did not have a company of men with whom he has since kept company—at least, not the men from the dedication page. As he says to Bruckner, "Well, yes, I dedicated the book to my characters. After all, I lived with them for five years while I was writing."

He says the book evolved as a "representation of the kinds of reality I lived through, but the picture is also changed by the dialogue, the storytelling technique, things I wasn't aware of at the time." He did have a friend who died as the result of a land mine, part of which was covered in his memoir, which reappeared with a new treatment in *The Things They Carried.* Part of it was also written in the field, while he was in Vietnam.

But, despite the eyewitness reality conveyed by many of the pieces, little was actually written in Vietnam. O'Brien said he didn't write much in the field because "words didn't seem adequate to the experience. I had this thing with drowning and gore and blood and terror, and words seemed superfluous ... but now and then I was overwhelmed and did start writing. What I'm trying to say, though, is that there was nothing conscious going on. I wasn't looking for literary material."

Somewhere between the inadequacy of language and the intensity of Vietnam's experience, O'Brien found the craft and technique to write *The Things They Carried*. As he does in all of his work, he had to find some means of breaking out of typical expectation to write about atypical moments. He decided that the Vietnam experience required immediacy, "an instant sort of pressure." He thus understood that typical, linear plot would not approximate the discursive and recurring nature of the war. At the same time, he needed to include a sense of what *things* were there. He has said that the death of animals recurs in his thoughts and experiences (he did, like his narrator, Tim, work in a meat packing plant the summer before he went to Vietnam), and he has also said that multiple perspectives and narrators help to atomize truth into something with pieces in everything, no single piece of which is then the whole truth. Between the scraps of dialogue that became whole people, the games of names and biography, and the non-linear techniques, Tim O'Brien fashioned a thoroughly surreal and invented story that writers, readers, and critics have described as one of the most real, convincing, and blunt portrayals of Vietnam put on paper. The paradox, then, too, is one of the things his characters carry.

List of Characters

Lt. Jimmy Cross is the reluctant and conflicted leader of the eighteen-man squad humping along the Song Tra Bong River. He is barely into his twenties, barely more together than his men. When Ted Lavender is killed, Cross feels responsible because at the time he was fantasizing about a woman from home, Martha. Afterward, Jimmy swears that the men will return to SOP (standard operating procedures), pull their act together, and behave responsibly. It doesn't help. Soon, Curt Lemon is killed by a landmine, and further aggravating Cross's guilt, the young lieutenant feels Lemon's death, too, was preventable. Finally, when he mistakenly camps the men in a shit field near the Song Tra Bong and the site is shelled by the Viet Cong, Kiowa is killed, and Jimmy feels the brunt of meaninglessness, despair, and guilt, especially when he contrasts it with the mute and numb reaction of the young soldier, Tim.

Curt Lemon is killed by a land mine, during an odd moment of play, when the narrator of the stories mused on how, at times, the war could be almost beautiful. The fact that Lemon dies when he does serves to underscore the absurd extremes in which the characters lived, and the moments which the characters would carry with them for years afterward. Lemon's death also inspires Rat Kiley to write a letter to Curt's sister, telling her what a great guy her brother was. When she doesn't write back, Kiley dismisses her.

Ted Lavender is a gentle soldier, at one point adopting a small puppy and nursing it to health with his own rations. His gentleness is exaggerated by his frequent use of tranquilizers and "premium dope." He is shot in the head after peeing in the jungle, and his death is a central concern for many of the characters.

Rat Kiley is an inveterate liar, and thus a frequent storyteller. However, he narrates one of the most discussed stories in *The*

Things They Carried, "Sweetheart of the Song Tra Bong," a combination of hearsay, foggy eyewitness accounts, speculation, and falsehood—all with the assertion and feel of truth. Rat is the medic for the company until he is wounded and shipped back to a hospital, to be replaced by Bobby Jorgenson. Rat is great friends with Curt Lemon, who is killed early on in the book. Rat kills a baby water buffalo, slowly, torturously, in pain after Lemon's death. Rat writes a long letter to Lemon's sister, telling of his admiration and affection for the woman's brother, and is disappointed when "the dumb cooze never [writes] back."

Kiowa is partly American Indian. His death in the shit field near the Song Tra Bong is one of the two central moments of conflict in *The Things They Carried*. Kiowa is perhaps the most spiritual of the characters, and a manifestation of conscience for the group. When Curt Lemon dies, Kiowa wants to talk about it, and after Ted Lavender's death, he also wants some means of marking the passing. He maintains a strong Christian belief as well as respect for the American Indian beliefs and animus of his mother. His carrying moccasins and a hunting hatchet as well as a New Testament in his rucksack represents adherence to the twin beliefs.

Tim O'Brien is both a character (the book's main narrator) as well as the author. The book maintains that the author and character are one; the author has maintained publicly and in interviews following the book's publication that the Tim O'Brien in the actual book is a character. The Tim O'Brien of the book is an author in his mid-forties who has written at least one other very successful book on the Vietnam experience, *Going After Cacciato*. He has a nine-year-old daughter, Katherine, whom he takes to Vietnam, to the place where her father feels he allowed his friend Kiowa to die. He also suffers a nearly fatal wound in the field, resulting in his convalescence and distance from the rest of the men in his company. His last breakdown is when he attempts to avenge his sense of alienation, which he pins squarely on Bobby Jorgenson. He enlists Azar to help him. When he feels he and Azar have pushed the attack too far, he suffers an anxiety attack.

Azar is described by Lorrie N. Nelson as "ridiculously macho." Indeed, Azar is the embodiment of the swaggering, warmongering male stereotype. But he is also aware of it. When he straps Ted Lavender's adopted puppy to an explosive device and detonates it, he says, "What's everybody so upset about? Christ, I'm just a *boy*." Azar agrees to help Tim act out a revenge on Bobby Jorgenson, but when Tim refuses to let the prank escalate to something truly vicious and damaging, Azar ridicules him and beats him.

Norman Bowker circles the lake in his hometown, in Iowa, almost ten times, in the episode "Speaking of Courage." His revolutions are seen as a metaphor for the aimlessness and pointlessness felt by many returning veterans in the years after Vietnam. He receives little attention in the rest of the episodes of the book, and is scarcely drawn. "Speaking of Courage" makes Bowker the soldier who, failing to help Kiowa, allows him to die in the shit field. However, later accounts make it clear that Tim is the one saddled with Kiowa's death. The question arises: is Bowker a stand-in for the possible stories Tim might have told?

Bobby Jorgenson is the green medic who replaces Rat Kiley after he's wounded and sent out of the country for R&R. Jorgenson freezes when Tim takes a bullet in the ass, and even after he gets to the wounded man, doesn't treat him for shock. He is the focus of much of Tim's antipathy. Not only does Jorgenson nearly kill Tim in the bush, but also his inaction aggravated the wound and made it necessary for Tim to recuperate, thereby in effect leaving the camaraderie of the soldiers. Tim and Jorgenson come to an understanding only after Tim, with the help of Azar, attempt to terrorize the man and it backfires, leaving Tim more terrorized than anyone else.

Henry Dobbins is repeatedly described as a big man who, despite his size, moves quite gracefully. He wears his girlfriend's stockings around his neck when he goes on patrol, and O'Brien describes him, at one point, as "like America itself, big and strong, full of good intentions, a roll of fat jiggling at his belly, slow of foot but always plodding along, always there when you needed him, a believer in the virtues of simplicity and directness and hard labor."

Dave Jensen and Lee Strunk are two soldiers who come to trust one another after a savage fistfight starting from Jensen accusing Strunk of theft. Their uneasy alliance forms the core of two episodes: "Friends" and "Enemies."

Mitchell Sanders is seldom seen without his yo-yo. Its appearance is like a nervous tic in a story, after something horrific, as when Rat Kiley kills the baby water buffalo. Sanders takes out the yo-yo afterward, and as the men all say they had seen nothing before like what Rat did, Sanders says, "Well, that's Nam ... Garden of Evil. Over here, man, every sin's real fresh and original."

Summary and Analysis

It starts right on the dedication page. It reads, "This book is lovingly dedicated to the men of Alpha Company, and in particular to Jimmy Cross, Norman Bowker, Rat Kiley, Mitchell Sanders, Henry Dobbins, and Kiowa." The dedication page, in some editions, sits across from the copyright page, on which is printed the usual disclaimer, albeit slightly tweaked: "This is a work of fiction. Except for a few details regarding the author's own life, all the incidents, names, and characters are imaginary."

Note how it does not say this *book*. Rather, the first pronoun, "This," is ambiguous, and could even refer to the disclaimer statement itself. O'Brien's classic work of Vietnam War literature inspires such games of intent by its readers. Throughout *The Things They Carried*, the notions of truth, story, fiction, and imagination are challenged by the way in which the story contradicts itself while featuring a narrator character that, biographically and nominally, is a clone of the author. And yet, Tim O'Brien has asserted in numerous interviews that the work is entirely made up. He even asserts it within the book. Scholars have pointed out that such ontological games are part of O'Brien's intentional commentary on the ontological game that was the war in Vietnam.

On its surface, the book is a collection of episodes dealing with the men who comprise one squad of Alpha Company. The book tells of the "things they carried," and as such tells of the literal items—photographs and rations and socks and so on—as well as the various weights and less tangible items—stories, memories, hopes, curses, guilts, and associations. The cumulative effect of the episodes is the reader's understanding of what the men endured, how they changed, and, to an extent, how things turned out at the conclusion of U.S. presence in Southeast Asia. A summary is perhaps most useful if it takes up each episode, building to become an overview of their collective effect.

A note on some terms: because the book is neither convincingly a novel or stories, it is hard to tell by what term one should refer to the pieces contained within it. Are they chapters? Are they stories? I will use the term "episode," reflecting, I hope, that the pieces are part of a loose whole, but a wholeness more diffracted than the use of the word "chapters" would suggest. As well, the term does not depend on the veracity of the pieces, on whether they are or are not fictive.

The Things They Carried

Bobbie Ann Mason, author of *In Country* and other novels and a writer whose work, like O'Brien's, frequently addresses the Vietnam War, writes about the opening episode of *The Things They Carried*:

> The immediate drama is the effort—by the main character, by the narrator, by the writer himself—to contain the emotion, to carry it. When faced with a subject almost too great to manage or confront, the mind wants to organize, to categorize, to simplify. Restraint and matter-of-factness are appropriate deflective techniques for dealing with pain, and they work on several levels in the story. Sometimes it is more affecting to see someone dealing with pain than it is to know about the pain itself. That's what's happening here ...
>
> His [Cross's, O'Brien's] effort to detach and control becomes both the drama and the technique of the story. For it is our impulse to deal with unspeakable horror and sadness by fashioning some kind of order, a story, to clarify and contain our emotions.[1]

Mason outlines the techniques of both the writer and the soldiers that will come to dominate the book—order, matter-of-factness, deflection, and the idea of story—and which are given, in the opinion of many, their highest expression in the opening episode.

The book's opening episode concerns the first death experienced by the whole of Alpha Company. While it is made clear later that Rat Kiley had experienced deaths before, the story implies that the majority of Alpha Company had not and, in particular, that it was the first such death experience for Kiowa, Tim, Norman Bowker, Mitchell Sanders, and, most importantly, for Lieutenant Jimmy Cross.

While this episode is the only one in the book to maintain a nearly omniscient narration, Jimmy Cross emerges as the main character. It is, after all, mostly his story. The first sentence: "First Lieutenant Jimmy Cross carried letters from a girl named Martha, a junior at Mount Sebastian College in New Jersey." The episode goes on to detail the optimistic detachment of the letters and how, to Jimmy, they become unintentional love letters. Some nights, sitting in his foxhole, holding the pictures in his fingers, he imagines a complete life with Martha, a life antithetical to the experience he was undergoing. The letters, at first, seem frivolous, especially as the passages which follow their excerpts detail the various official items the soldiers carried: rations, watches, dog tags, and a litany of specifics issued by the U.S. military, each with a specific purpose and reason for encumbering the soldiers. The sentimental reasons for carrying letters from a girl, in comparison, are slight. But other items soon enter the list, mentioned alongside military issue gear, and presented as necessities, talismans, and character traits:

> Ted Lavender carried six or seven ounces of premium dope, which for him was a necessity. Mitchell Sanders, the RTO, carried condoms. Norman Bowker carried a diary. Rat Kiley carried comic books. Kiowa, a devout Baptist, carried an illustrated New Testament that had been presented to him by his father, who taught Sunday school in Oklahoma City, Oklahoma. As a hedge against bad times, however, Kiowa also carried his grandmother's distrust of the white man, his grandfather's old hunting hatchet. Necessity dictated.

Juxtaposition and litany are the two main techniques in the first story. The litany reifies the sense of constancy the men experienced: constant conditions, constant fear and apprehension, constant movement, and constant burdens. The list form repeats and circles in on itself. With each new rough rotation, readers go through the list of men and learn more and more. And as the list grows, the juxtapositions help to tell the story of Ted Lavender's death and its effect on the squad, interrupting the mundane explanations and items with the sudden insistence of loss:

> Because the nights were cold, and because the monsoons were wet, each carried a green plastic poncho that could be used as a raincoat or groundsheet or makeshift tent. With its quilted liner, the poncho weighed almost two ounces, but it was worth every ounce. In April, for instance, when Ted Lavender was shot, they used his poncho to wrap him up, then to carry him across the paddy, then to lift him into the chopper that took him away.

The story tells the absurd and violent tale of Ted Lavender's getting shot on returning from peeing in the jungle. Lavender was scared, and the story implies that his fear had something to do with his fate. (By contrast, Azar, a macho type, is the one character in the book that seems to escape from any harm.) The reactions of the men at once reveal personal trauma and group coping. On an individual level, the men have many reactions. Kiowa keeps muttering about the death, keeps repeating the same few lines about how suddenly and completely Lavender fell: "I swear to God—boom, down. Not a word." Norman Bowker keeps telling him to shut up, to stop talking, until, finally frustrated, he tells Kiowa to talk, and the man says nothing. (Later, in "Speaking of Courage," Bowker himself will want to talk, and will have no one he *can* talk to.) Rat Kiley moves through the next few days, saying again and again, "*hey, he's dead, he's really dead.*" Jimmy Cross himself feels a horrible burden for the death itself, which will be discussed more in a moment. However, for all their personal trauma over the death of Lavender, as a group they move him to the chopper site and, once there, "sat smoking the dead man's dope until the chopper came."

Readers learn gradually in the story that Jimmy Cross holds himself responsible for Lavender's death. He feels he was distracted, daydreaming while on patrol in the jungle. Instead of eyeing the perimeter and keeping abreast of the positions of his men, he imagined himself barefoot on a beach in New Jersey with Martha, a women whose love for him he knows is entirely imagined, but to him feels, until Lavender's death, no less real. Cross's invented story resonates with the metafictional project O'Brien the author is undertaking with *The Things They Carried*. In this case, the story Cross has made up is so powerfully real to him that it has consequences in the real world, and articulates his hurt and distance in ways more persuasive than his assertions would ever be.

The tension of the story builds in two ways. First, through the simple mechanics of the story. Readers know Lavender dies long before they understand how. That information is delivered piecemeal, heightening dramatic tension. The second way in which tension is built is through the more metaphorical aspects of the list of things they carried. "They all carried ghosts," readers are told at one point. At another time, "Often, they carried each other, the wounded or weak. They carried infections ... They carried the land itself—Vietnam, the place, the soil—a powdery orange-red dust that covered their boots and fatigues and faces." "They carried all the emotional baggage of men who might die." As well, "for all the ambiguities of Vietnam, all the mysteries and unknowns, there was at least the single abiding certainty that they would never be at a loss for things to carry."

With Jimmy Cross as the focus, the first story, then, is about how Lavender's death gave him one more thing to carry, one of particular weight. Kiowa sees it, and wishes he could bear some of the burden for Cross. None of the other men talk about it. Cross himself knows he can no longer fantasize about Martha, about her love, or any of it. He says, to himself, "No more fantasies." His new weight, in spite of his simultaneous new resolve, will have its effect. As O'Brien writes, "Grief, terror, love, longing—these were intangibles, but the intangibles had their own mass and specific gravity, they had tangible weight." Cross's weight—guilt over Lavender—makes him burn the photos and letters, chew out the platoon, restore standard operating procedures, and face the war with new resolve. The stories that follow bear out how little such resolve matters.

Love

Immediately following the title story, the episode appears at first autobiographical, wherein the "real" Jimmy Cross goes to visit "Tim," who is now a writer. The "Tim" writer seems in every respect identical to Tim O'Brien. Many years after the war, Tim is living in Massachusetts, and when Jimmy visits, the two talk about "all the things we still carry through our lives." They look at snapshots, drink, smoke a bit, and remember some of the things carried in the war.

Jimmy shows Tim a photo of Martha. In the previous episode, Cross had burned the photo, and when Tim asks him about it, we learn that Jimmy has gotten a new one from Martha herself; he saw her at a reunion in 1979. The Martha of this story has, of course, moved on, married, with a family of her own. But not without trouble. Jimmy relates that she has changed, that her eyes are now "gray," and that when he tells her, half in jest, about how he had decided he should have tied her to the bed on a first date and touched only her knee again and again, she is disturbed. She says she doesn't understand how "men could do those things." For her, the question is as pointed as it is for the reader: how can they kill, obsess, laugh about it, die, and keep going?

Jimmy is still aware of the power of story, and when he learns Tim is thinking of making a story of their experiences, wonders if, assuming the tale is well told, it won't send Martha running to him. Then, Cross realizes what might well be included, the responsibility, the deaths of Lavender, and, later, Kiowa, and Cross's complicity in both situations. He says to

Tim, "Don't mention anything about—" and Tim's response, "Never," is immediately undercut by the evidence.

The small episode introduces several sustaining themes of the book: the guilt the men all carried, the question of complicity in heinous acts, the difference in understanding between those who fought and those who stayed home, and even, as one critic herein discusses, the role of women in the tale. It also plays with truth in ways that several other sections will build upon.

Spin

"Spin" tells a set of anecdotes all meant to show, as the "Tim" says, "The war wasn't all terror and violence. Sometimes things could almost get sweet." Immediately after the statement, Tim gives us an example of that sweetness, a one-legged boy hopping over to ask Azar for a candy bar. Azar announces afterward, "War's a bitch ... One leg, for Chrissake. Some poor fucker ran out of ammo." The passage juxtaposes readers' usual ideas about what constitutes "sweet" with this different understanding.

Each little story throughout the "Spin" episode works the same way. Ted Lavender only calls the war "mellow" when he takes too many tranquillizers. Norman Bowker and Henry Dobbins enjoy checkers because there are clear rules and a clear winner. Mitchell Sanders provides the men a moment of twisted levity when he mails an envelope of his own body lice back to his draft board.

Because the humor is redefined, so too is everything else about the war. The writer, Tim, tells readers that now, as a writer, at age 43, much of the war is hard to remember. He talks about how the "bad stuff" is always replaying itself and that, even though such moments are the dominant images—the majority of what is remembered and, thus, *carried*—they are not all of it. "The war wasn't all that way." However, because the moments of lightness are so terrible, readers realize it's all bad, regardless of what the narrator says. In this way, the narrator begins to become unreliable. The rest of the story bears this out.

When the narrator describes the boredom of waiting, he contrasts it with the raw-nerve work of humping. He writes,

> You'd be sitting at the top of a high hill, the flat paddies stretching out below, and the day would be calm and hot and utterly vacant, and you'd feel the boredom dripping inside you like a leaky faucet, except it wasn't water, it was a sort of acid, and with each little droplet you'd feel the stuff eating away at important organs. You'd try to relax. You'd uncurl your fists and let your thoughts go. Well, you'd think, this isn't so bad. And right then you'd hear gunfire behind you and your nuts would fly up into your throat and you'd be squealing pig squeals. That kind of boredom.

Peace stories have details like an AWOL soldier returning to fight because, while gone, he experiences peace, and ends up wanting to "hurt the peace back." Or Azar blowing up Ted Lavender's adopted puppy, and his own self-awareness and understanding of consequence and maturity ("What's everybody so upset about? ... Christ, I'm just a *boy*.") When Tim concedes that some of the stories (and, by implication, some of the author's own) are made up, he says they still gave him "a quick truth-goose." It *felt* real. At the end of the story, the narrator revisits that point. He tells how remembering things leads to stories that are bigger than the things themselves. "Stories are for joining the past to the future," he says. "Stories are for eternity, when memory is erased, when there is nothing to remember except the story."

The effects of "Spin" are, to take the title literally, a spin on the truth. However true to its sources O'Brien's work remains, this episode acknowledges that even the sources, even the war itself and the men and the things they carried, are tainted by interpretation, stories, twisted understandings of things like peace, boredom, sweetness, and even truth. The story tells how it is all spin, art and life alike.

Further, it begins to reveal the circular pattern of the narration itself. The deaths of Lavender and Kiowa are both foreshadowed and retold here, placing the story in several different temporal areas. The technique is used again and again in *The Things They Carried*, in effect spinning the tale and returning us to notions of truth again and again.

On the Rainy River; Enemies; Friends

"On the Rainy River" is the only episode to occur entirely before the war. The piece conflates two identities that, in the years after Vietnam, developed into archetypes for the period: the draftee who flees to Canada, and the guilt- or duty-bound young man who goes and fights, however reluctantly or fearfully. When the narrator writes, "This is one story I've never told before," it suggests any of several reasons. Readers come to learn that the narrator's reluctance may stem from what he perceives as revealing weakness: his emotional breakdown, his lack of courage actually to desert, and a fear of his family and friends learning of his weakness.

The story is also a meditation on heroism, something the book returns to implicitly many times, asking what constitutes heroism. O'Brien the narrator says, "All of us, I suppose, like to believe that in a moral emergency we will behave like the heroes of our youth, bravely and forthrightly, without thought of personal loss or credit." Repeatedly, the men of Alpha Company fail to do so. Tim himself fails to act at the time of Kiowa's death and, although it's doubtful his actions would have made a difference, blames himself for the loss. In the two episodes immediately following "Rainy River," Lee Strunk and Dave Jensen fight over Jensen's accusing Strunk of stealing his jackknife. Strunk denies it, though we learn that he actually did. Jensen, the physically bigger man, breaks Strunk's nose in the lopsided fistfight that ensues. Strunk continues to deny stealing the knife, even while Jensen mentally flogs himself with worry over Strunk's possible revenge. A few days later, After Jensen breaks his own nose with a pistol butt, just to make things "square," Strunk acknowledges—though never to

Jensen—that he *did* steal the knife. Neither man's behavior is exactly "conduct becoming," even for a grunt.

But the episode that follows, "Friends," details how the two men learned to trust one another. When a mine takes off Strunk's leg, Jensen rides with him in the chopper as the wounded man moves in and out of consciousness. He pleads that Jensen not kill him, presumably worried that Jensen would want to put him out of his misery. Jensen does not, but as the narrator tells readers, when Strunk does actually die later, in another transport, Jensen seems relieved of "an enormous weight."

The behaviors are not the kinds one might hold up as examples of courage or rectitude, unless one considers the last line of "Friends." The enormous weight is not articulated, but readers can intuit that Jensen's experiences with Strunk as well as his cock-eyed sense of moral balance led him to feel somehow responsible for Strunk. Theirs was a camaraderie O'Brien the writer reveals in different ways throughout the book. In its unusual way of defining courage—taking responsibility for the welfare of another—then "Rainy River" itself might reveal a variety of courage as valid as the more typical, hero-story portrayal.

In "On the Rainy River," Tim graduates from a small college and is drafted into a war he "hated." It seems wrong, and he doesn't know whom or what to trust. The draft notice causes him to fear, and then to rationalize the many reasons he could not go to war. They cover the range of thought others have covered regarding war, culminating in the narrator's conviction that, if a person was for a war, "You have to head for the front and hook up with an infantry unit and help spill the blood. And you have to bring along your wife, your kids, or your lover."

He worked in a slaughterhouse that summer, a convenient metaphor, however autobiographical it might be. His job was a "Declotter," ensuring that the decapitated pig carcasses would bleed out by hosing away blood clots that formed at the neck and upper chest cavity. He stunk of gore and pig all the time. He would spend evenings driving around town— foreshadowing the hopeless, meaningless laps Norman Bowker will drive after the war, in a later story. While driving, he would think of ways to elude the draft, but there were no options. He states that, were it a just war, he'd have no problem signing up. He says, "The problem, though, was that a draft board did not let you choose your war."

He decides to run. At this point, he concedes that he has told parts of this tale, but has never told the entire truth of it, how he cracked, how he lacked some part of himself that would have allowed him to flee entirely, crossing the Canadian border and not looking back. He drives north and, meeting up with Minnesota's Rainy River, the natural feature dividing Minnesota from Canada, follows it west through wilderness, looking for a place to cross. Exhausted and scared, he stops at the Tip Top Lodge, and is taken into the company of Elroy Burdahl, the owner, and sole occupant at the time.

Elroy is reticent, maintaining a "willful, almost ferocious silence." Tim figures the man knows why an American boy of draft age would be near the border in the middle of the week. Still, Burdahl says nothing about it. Burdahl, Tim claims, "is the hero of my life." They take meals together for six days, play Scrabble, hike, and generally pass the time. Tim knows Burdahl understands his trouble, and that he is struggling with it. At one point, he brings up the bill to Tim, and as he figures it and the total climbs, he tells Tim that he also needs to figure labor compensation for the odd jobs Tim has done—stacking wood, cleaning dishes, and the like. Burdahl calculates a generous wage, resulting in Tim's being paid by Burdahl rather than owing him money. Tim won't take it, and so goes to bed with the money lying on the table. The next morning, when he enters the kitchen for breakfast, the money is in an envelope on which Burdahl has written EMERGENCY FUND. Tim says, "The man knew."

On Tim's last day at the lodge, Burdahl takes him fishing. The two take a motorboat out on the river, and soon they are at the Canadian edge. Burdahl waits for Tim to decide, busying himself with his tackle box and otherwise preparing to fish.

As the old man waits him out, Tim feels the weight of his decision, describes it as a "tightness." The moment is another when fact and fiction blur—"Even now, as I write this, I can still feel the tightness."—as well as one where the author purposely confronts the reader, asking for participation in what he insists is fiction. He writes:

> What would you do?
> Would you jump? Would you feel pity for yourself? Would you think about your family and your childhood and your dreams and all you're leaving behind? Would it hurt? Would it feel like dying? Would you cry, as I did?
> I tried to swallow it back. I tried to smile, except I was crying.
> Now, perhaps, you can understand why I've never told this story before. It's not just the embarrassment of tears. That's part of it, no doubt, but what embarrasses me much more, and always will, is the paralysis that took my heart. A moral freeze: I couldn't decide, I couldn't act, I couldn't comport myself with even a pretense of modest human dignity.

Among tales that ask how men can commit atrocities, how they can *decide* to be monstrous, this tale's meditation on cowardice and courage of indecision stands out. The reverie which follows is a foretelling and a retrospective, a vision of the actions of wars past and yet to come, "chunks of [his] own history" as well as the United States Senate, a girl who died of a brain tumor, "LBJ, and Huck Finn, and Abbie Hoffman" and, later, Jimmy Cross, who he cannot yet possibly know of. In the choking reverie, he has a hallucinatory moment of clarity, but even that moment freezes his actions. To Tim, the reverie is all those watching, all those who are waiting for him to fight, all those who would find him an embarrassment if he did not. Tim's failure to act is due to a fear of embarrassment, and is thus cowardice. He does not feel indecision due to the complexity of the war or duty or anything else. He makes it clear: his chief motivation, at that moment, was to avoid embarrassment, thereby violating the very recently evolved principals he had against the war.

Burdahl makes no mention of it, and simply returns to the lodge. The next morning, Tim wakes, sees no sign of the man other than more money left for him, which he doesn't take. He leaves, then, "to Vietnam, where I was a soldier, and then home again. I survived, but it's not a happy ending. I was a coward. I went to the war."

Later, readers will also learn that he considers his actions in the war itself largely to be cowardly: his killing a soldier in an ambush, and his complicity in the death of Kiowa. Cowardice and its complicated forms are what haunt this narrator. Thus, what makes Burdahl his hero is that he takes Tim to face himself, to face the enormity of both desertion and fighting.

How To Tell A True War Story

By this point in the book, O'Brien has not played many truth games. Only the episode "Spin" mentions any of the ideas around truth, memorably using the term "truth-goose" to relate how a story unlikely to be factually true still resonated with those that heard it. The episode, "How To Tell A True War Story," however, makes much play of truth.

It starts, "This is true." The claim has its own line and paragraph, setting it off from the rest of the tale, a dramatic promise for any storyteller to make, and one that often heightens the impact or calls for special attention on the part of the reader. And it almost always presages something that is nearly unbelievable, thereby requiring the teller's assurance that it is true.

In this case, however, as the story evolves it seems the admonishment is not so much due to the unbelievable quality of the story but to its layered quality. Various narrators "tell" the story, each remembering different versions, and the episode tries to contain those perspectives while going after an individual true-ness. At the opener, we learn the simple story: Rat Kiley is best friends with Curt Lemon. One day in the jungle, a mine explodes and kills Lemon. Rat writes to Lemon's sister, to tell her what a great guy her brother was. Rat tells of his admiration and affection for the other soldier. He waits two months for a reply. There is none.

Basically, that is the end of the story. But it is far from the end of the episode. Instead, O'Brien proceeds to outline why the anecdote is both a "true" war story, and a proper war story. He tells the reader, "A true war story is never moral." The claim explains O'Brien's resistance to epiphany, to resolution, to "closure," or any other finite sense in the narrative, and it explains the episodic, non-definitive quality of the book, as well as its enduring power to shock and disgust:

> It does not instruct, nor encourage virtue, nor suggest models of proper human behavior, nor restrain men from doing the things men have always done. If a story seems moral, do not believe it. If at the end of a war story you feel uplifted, or if you feel that some small bit of rectitude has been salvaged from the larger waste, then you have been made the victim of a very old and terrible lie. There is no rectitude whatsoever. There is no virtue. As a first rule of thumb, therefore, you can tell a true war story by its absolute and uncompromising allegiance to obscenity and evil. Listen to Rat Kiley. Cooze, he says. He does not say bitch. He certainly does not say woman, or girl. He says cooze. Then he spits and stares. He's nineteen years old—it's too much for him— so he looks at you with those big sad gentle killer eyes and says *cooze*, because his friend is dead, and because it's so incredibly sad and true: she never wrote back.

O'Brien then imagines the death of Lemon as he remembers it, and the writing here describes a moment of beauty. Lyric sentences evoke nature. Rat and Curt are playing catch with a smoke grenade, a game they've devised, turning weaponry into amusement. O'Brien describes the moment of Lemon's death as the sunlight coming and lifting him up, "high into a tree full of moss and vines and white blossoms." The constancy of juxtaposition is at work here again: play with weapons, truth with memory, death with natural beauty, love with obscenity.

O'Brien then asserts, "In many cases, a true war story cannot be believed." He proceeds to retell a story Mitchell Sanders told. A patrol goes deep into the jungle, and they are there for six days, scared, quiet, listening. They begin to hear things—strange voices, murmurs, and music—and after a few days, the sounds grow to them more specific until, on the sixth night, they hear chamber music, martini glasses, and the sounds of a complete and raucous party. They think it's the jungle, the place, the whole country. As Sanders says, "The whole country. Vietnam. The place talks. It talks. Understand? Nam—it truly talks."

Then, as Sanders says, they lose it. Calling in support, they report movement of an entire enemy army. The air force brings in napalm. Extra infantry arrives. Artillery and gun ships shell the coordinates. Once the area is demolished, according to Sanders, the soldiers still hear the sound. When a colonel comes to ask about the excessive order of force and the cost, the men say nothing.

> They just look at him for a while, sort of funny like, sort of amazed, and the whole war is right in that stare. It says everything you can't ever say. It says, man, you got *wax* in your ears. It says, poor bastard, you'll never know—wrong frequency—you don't *even* want to hear this. Then they salute the fucker and walk away, because certain stories you don't ever tell.

"You can tell a true war story the way it never seems to end," O'Brien writes. "Not then, not ever." The claim matches the circularity of the book and its episodes. The deaths of Lavender and Lemon are revisited several times, with details imagined differently, or re-imagined, or re-interpreted. Kiowa is an undercurrent of conscience and humanity, and is killed, as the episode's guidelines suggest he should be. And the complex make-up of "Tim" is continually revisited, whether in fact or fiction, by the simple creation and existence of the book.

O'Brien the writer even undercuts the guidelines for war stories themselves. As soon as Sanders finishes the story,

O'Brien comments that Sanders regretted how he didn't get it all right. Then, later in the night, Sanders comes to O'Brien to tell him the moral. This moment comes just paragraphs after the author had told the reader not to trust anything with a moral. Sanders' moral is that "you got to listen to your enemy." In the next paragraph, Sanders concedes that he had to "make up a few things." But he insists it was still true. To Sanders, the detail embellishment served to underscore the sheer oddity of what the men thought they had encountered. Tim understands this, and then asks Sanders what the moral is. When Sanders asks Tim to listen to the quiet, assuring him that's where the moral is, the episode turns back to its stringent guidelines. The moral is nothing, the sound that can't be heard, silence, non-existent. Or, it's the fullness of what might be heard. Either way, it is not set, definitive, *there* in any conventional sense.

But the episode then circles one more time. O'Brien says, "In a true war story, if there's a moral at all, it's like the thread that makes the cloth. You can't tease it out, you can't extract the meaning without unraveling the deeper meaning. And in the end, really, there's nothing much to say about a war story, except maybe 'Oh.'" O'Brien's insistence on the medium being the message is further compromised when he mentions that a true war story never generalizes. Yet the reader is experiencing a war story that, on every page, asserts its veracity, however codified and ironically, while maintaining a list of generalizations about war stories and, thus, war. In the episodes that surround this one, details are given without comment, without moral, and without a care for consistency. They are, perhaps, difficult to believe because of their inconsistencies, their familiarity when read against other stories, or their simple emergence by and large from hearsay. Yet, if they are incredible, without reductive statements of a moral, and without a point but that which resonates abstractly in the gut, then they meet the litmus test for truth. In that sense, then, this episode might be read as the author's apologia.

In the third and final section of the episode, O'Brien revisits Lemon's death again, asserting, "here's what actually happened." Rat, in response to Lemon's death (or so the placement of the tale suggests), tortures and kills a baby water buffalo by shooting it, a single round at a time, in several places, before switching his gun to automatic and spraying the animal with bullets. Finally, after squatting before it and putting the final round through the animal's nose, he leaves, crying. O'Brien's episode has virtually no response to Rat's deed. Instead, the piece goes on about how it is nearly impossible to generalize, since war comprises so many experiences, "hell ... mystery and terror and adventure and courage and discovery and holiness and pity and despair and longing and love ... The truths are contradictory." The implication, thus, is that truth itself contradicts what we learn to expect of things that are "true." As the saw goes, truth is stranger than fiction.

As O'Brien goes over the deaths again, tells of more details—Dave Jensen singing "Lemon Tree" as they threw down Curt's body parts from the trees, or of the grenade story that's "a true story that never happened"—truth gets fuzzier and fuzzier. When he tells about women enjoying the story when he reads it—again reminding readers of the authorial hand at work—and telling him he needs to find more stories to tell, he thinks about all the ways it could change, *has* changed, or might change, how it might have happened somewhere else, or how it never happened, and how he realizes it's a love story, perhaps. In all of the spinning about the story, he reiterates the central claims of the episode: that it be pointless, that it be unbelievable, that it be endless, that it be contradictory. That it might simply be.

The Dentist

Lest Curt Lemon be too deified, the author gives readers the next episode, "The Dentist," wherein Lemon is described. Tim did not like him. He played the tough soldier, pulled dangerous stunts, went trick-or-treating naked with only a mask one Halloween in a small village in the jungle. He "kept replaying his won exploits." O'Brien writes, "it's easy to get sentimental about the dead, and to guard against that I want to tell a quick Curt Lemon story."

In short, Lemon had bad experiences with dentists. When the company had to see one, Lemon fainted right away. Nothing more happened. Later that night, though, unsatisfied with not having experienced the trauma he thought he should have, Lemon woke up the dentist, told him he had a toothache, and convinced the man to pull a perfectly health tooth. The next day Lemon was "all smiles."

The episode is one of the many short pieces placed between the longer episodes, almost as comic or psychic relief to the depth and Byzantine turns of the longer pieces. But they are not all humorous, nor are they all simply anecdotal. Some of them are powerful despite their size. But the cumulative effect of such undercutting and repackaging of powerful material is to break the pace, to upset expectation even within the book. The technique is a rough approximation of the action of the book. Move, think, wait, die, move, die, wait, and so on.

Sweetheart of the Song Tra Bong

The opening episode of the book, "The Things They Carried," depends on a (yet) unquestioned omniscience for its power, a view that could soar to 40,000 feet and yet still dive to rest right behind the eyes of a particular soldier. O'Brien does not start his "truth-goosing" until after the piece, so that all work afterward stems from that initial introductory tone. In "Sweetheart of the Song Tra Bong," however, the story is one told to the narrator (and other soldiers) by Rat Kiley, and one that, by this point of the story, after readers see Mitchell Sanders and others embellish stories, and after the narrator's own lengthy treatise on truth, depends on its narration in a different way. "Sweetheart" is supposed to leave us with doubts, mysteries, and a lack of answers, partly due to the narrator's unreliability. As well, because Rat is able to comment throughout on the story's meaning and structure, he heightens the feeling of artifice. Still, despite Rat's groping for a "point" or "moral," "Sweetheart" meets all the criteria of a "true" war story: it is incredible, it never ends, it circles back on itself, and it contradicts—itself, expectations, and the narrator. Additionally, despite *Rat's* search for a moral, the story never yields one, thus adhering to another of the guidelines O'Brien has set down for "true" war stories.

The narrator deals right away with the story's incredible quality:

Rat has a reputation for exaggeration and overstatement, a compulsion to rev up the facts, and for most of us it was normal procedure to discount sixty or seventy percent of anything he had to say. If Rat told you, for example, that he'd slept with four girls one night, you could figure it was about a girl and a half. It wasn't a question of deceit. Just the opposite: he wanted to heat up the truth, to make it burn so hot that you would feel exactly what he felt. For Rat Kiley, I think, facts were formed by sensation, not the other way around, and when you listened to one of his stories, you'd find yourself performing rapid calculations in your head, subtracting superlatives, figuring the square root of absolute, then multiplying by maybe.

The story retells the tale of a young woman who arrives in Vietnam and winds up a savage warrior after several weeks of immersion. Eddie Diamond runs a medical detachment away from the full tumult of the war and a soldier, Mark Fossie, arranges to have his girlfriend flown in to the camp. She arrives, Rat says, "... with a suitcase and one of those plastic cosmetics bags ... she's got on culottes. White culottes and this sexy pink sweater. There she *is*."

Rat explains the curious circumstances that get her there—a bold and bored young soldier whose slight naiveté helps; a permissive NCO; little oversight; light to no fighting; a bureaucratic war machine easily manipulated; and time. She arrives in a camp where the party is a dull constant. The camp had once been a base for Green Beret operations when the United States was more covert about its involvements in

Southeast Asia, and one small group of six "Greenies" still inhabits a hootch at the camp's perimeter.

From the first, Mary Anne is a surprise. She gets along well with the soldiers, playing volleyball in cutoffs, dancing to tunes on a portable tape deck. But she is also curious. "The war intrigued her. The land, too, and the mystery." She wants to visit the village nearby and, when Fossie doesn't want to take her, she enlists Rat and two others. She loves it, even stops to swim in the Song Tra Bong, in her underwear, on the way back.

Rat pauses at this point in the story, and Tim notes to tell the reader that Rat was defensive of the details, quick to irk if questioned. And while the story seemed funny, "to hear Rat Kiley tell it you'd almost think it was intended as straight tragedy."

After the village visit, she begins to ask about more, to show a willingness to pitch in. She learns how to help when casualties arrive—clipping arteries, administering morphine. She soon falls "into the habits of the bush. No cosmetics, no fingernail filing ... hygiene [becomes] a matter of small consequence." As one critic points out, Mary Anne is the only female character in the book to enter the war, but not until she loses aspects of her character typically associated with female gendered behavior. As her transformation progresses, she learns to shoot, and she develops a new confidence in her voice and bearing. When Fossie suggests it might be time to go home, she asserts that everything she wants is there.

Eventually, she starts to stay out later during the night, not returning to Fossie or the tent. Then, "finally, she did not come in at all." Fossie can't find her one night. The soldiers scour the camp and turn up no sign of her. Only in the morning does she return—in the company of the six Greenies. One nods to her respectfully, another glares at Fossie. Otherwise, they say nothing. Mary Anne had been out on ambush.

While many of the episodes feature tales rejecting the violence of the war, or show men trying to deal with it through irony (Sanders) or machismo (Azar), only one character is shown to embrace it: Mary Anne. Some critics wonder at the significance of the one character being a woman, asking if O'Brien's message carries some commentary on the nature of women, one more subtle than its meditation on the nature of men. In the first episode, Lt. Cross looks at Martha and is able to contain "the things men carried inside. The things men did or felt they had to do." After the things Mary Anne, does, however, she is undone. So while the violence of her actions implies to Rat a kind of strength, it seems, in contrast, that O'Brien treats it as a kind of weakness.

After Fossie talks to Mary Anne and tells the men they are engaged, things are calm for a few days, until Mary Anne disappears again, unable to resist the draw. She leaves with the Greenies. She doesn't return for three weeks. When she does stroll back into camp, Rat says, it was like an "opium dream," and he says he thought he saw her eyes glowing, jungle green. Rat pauses at this point in the story, to "bracket the full range of meaning." He says:

"I know it sounds far-out," he'd tell us, "but it's not like *impossible* or anything. We all heard plenty of wackier stories. Some guy comes back from the bush, tells you he saw the Virgin Mary out there, she was riding a goddamn goose or something. Everybody buys it. Everybody smiles and asks how fast was they going, did she have spurs on. Well, it's not like that. This Mary Anne wasn't no virgin but at least she was real. I saw it. When she came in through the wire that night, I was right there, I saw those eyes of hers, I saw how she wasn't even the same person no more. What's so impossible about that? She was a girl, that's all. I mean, if it was a guy, everybody'd say, Hey, no big deal, he got caught up in the Nam shit, he got seduced by the Greenies. See what I mean? You got all these blinders on about women. How gentle and peaceful they are. All that crap about how if we had a pussy for president there wouldn't be no more wars. Pure garbage. You got to get rid of that sexist attitude."

Of course, Rat's invocation of the Virgin Mary as a standard invokes a kind of unconscious sexuality that makes the passage rather ironic in ways similar to the "nice" treatment espoused by Henry Dobbins in the episodes which follow (q.v.). O'Brien's undercutting Rat's moral in such a way also helps to bolster his contention regarding the *a*-morality of a true war story.

Fossie is now angry. He stations himself outside the Greenies' hootch and waits. He waits all day. That night, he hears a musical sound—a surreal sound similar in quality to the one described in the "How To Tell A True War Story" episode. Fossie knows it's Mary Anne and he wants to go into the hootch after her. The other soldiers appeal to his sense, as they all fear the mysterious Special Forces soldiers. But he won't be stopped. He barges into the tent and sees candles, smells rotting flesh and incense and joss sticks, hears more "tribal" music. He sees that the room is full of bones of all kinds, as well as a severed and rotting leopard head. The Greenies have hung a sign that reads, "ASSEMBLE YOUR OWN GOOK!! FREE SAMPLE KIT!!" He makes out the men on hammocks or crouched in the gloom, and then he sees Mary Anne.

She is dressed in her sweater and culottes, but she is a negative of the woman who had arrived weeks before. She wears a necklace of human tongues around her neck. She says to him, "You're in a place ... where you don't belong." She means more than just the tent or the camp. She means the war. She goes on to describe her "electric" connection to the war and its place. She says, "I know exactly who I am. You can't feel like that anywhere else." It is a sentiment that appears in a few spots in the book, referring to the intensity of war that becomes, while hellish, also addictive—the soldier who wanted to "hurt [the peace] back," or Norman Bowker's fruitless search for some similar intensity (q.v.). In Mary Anne's case, it signals not just a damaged person, as it does in the male characters. It signals a lost self entirely, as if there is no room for the original person to exist along with the changed one, as it seems to be in the male characters (Pamela Smiley (q.v.) discusses this in greater detail). As Rat tells Fossie, when the soldier says he can't let her go: "Man, you must be deaf. She's already gone."

And since a true war story can never end, this one does not. Rat tells the men, much to the consternation of Mitchell Sanders, that he never knew what happened to her. Of course, he had heard some things, from the Greenies in particular, told through Eddie Diamond, the layers of removal making the whole thing more incredulous. In the end, after Rat confessed that he "loved" Mary Anne, mainly because she was the one woman he could have talked to about the war who would have understood, he tells them what everyone suspected happened. The Greenies said she took pleasure in night patrol, took pleasure in getting lost in the war. And, in the end, that's what happened. She was swallowed up in it. Consumed. And she *was* the war. The final image reiterates the female difference, and is a twist on the classic femme fatale:

> She had crossed to the other side. She was part of the land. She was wearing her culottes, her pink sweater, and a necklace of human tongues. She was dangerous. She was ready for the kill.

Stockings and *Church; Style*

Both episodes deal with Henry Dobbins. The first simply explains the mysterious luck of Dobbins' girlfriend's pantyhose. He wears them around his neck and they protect him from harm. The men see it and, as Tim says, "You don't dispute facts." It is an odd causal relationship for a book in which one of the central tenets is that causality is artificial. The irony is that the book is all about disputing facts. But in this context, with Dobbins as a stand in for "America," the logical fallacy becomes commentary of a sort. If Dobbins is America, and the luck of the hosiery makes believers, then even when circumstances change (the girlfriend breaks it off in a letter) the hosiery still works. Put another way, if the role of American involvement in Vietnam is advisory, then regardless of the escalation of combat, the role is still advisory. The connection between Dobbins, America, and logical fallacy suggests O'Brien's political intent in the passage, despite the book's avoidance of moral.

Dobbins is not "bad," however, and neither is America portrayed as such. There is the affability, the good intent, and so on. O'Brien's connection is complicated. In the next episode, "Church," there is the same problem. Dobbins is unwittingly condescending to the monks who aid him in cleaning his weapon. As well, his joking with Kiowa about being an "Indian preacher ... [with] Feathers and buffalo robes" smacks of the pseudo-benevolent racist attitudes that some critics say have characterized much of American foreign policy in the twentieth century. But Dobbins' condescension is cast into highest relief when he tells Kiowa—who has serious moral reservations about cleaning their weapons and hunkering down in a church—"All you can do is be nice. Treat them decent, you know?" His "decent" treatment is to give each monk a can of peaches and a chocolate bar for cleaning the M-60, then telling them to beat it, to leave the pagoda. However, the monks seem to have little problem with it. The only one revealing any displeasure is Kiowa. The monks call Dobbins "soldier Jesus." Dobbins thinks he might join an order, "Find a monastery somewhere. Wear a robe and be nice to people." He acknowledges that religious leadership requires "brains," but he thinks he could handle being nice. Again, the resonance of intent without substance is powerful.

Between the previous episode's portrayal of the "sweetheart" and the one which follows, with the highly feminized description of the man the narrator killed, the two episodes together make for a link with strong undercurrents about imagining the American ethos as understood in the war, and as it has lingered in different ways since. The suggestion of a well-meaning feckless passive racist/sexist hegemony as typical of American ideals is something the book develops. O'Brien's several interviews bear out his intent. Still, Dobbins is not "bad."

Although it doesn't appear until later in the book, "Style" also features Henry Dobbins, behaving again like a well-meaning but not very sophisticated giant. In the story, a brief anecdote, the group comes upon a destroyed hamlet where a barefooted girl danced before a house wherein the rest of her family lay killed. Azar does not appreciate her grace, whereas Dobbins finds it intriguing. Azar writes her off as performing some ritual, but Dobbins suspects she "just likes to dance." Later, when Azar mocks the girl's dancing, Dobbins picks him up and holds him over a well, asking Azar if he'd like to be dropped in. Azar does not, to which Dobbins says, "All right then ... dance right."

The Man I Killed

Lorrie N. Moore (q.v.) notes how the description of the man Tim kills is "distinctly feminized, as if to underscore absolute otherness." It is only one of two detailed descriptions of "Viet persons" in the book, the other being a dancer in "Style." The author has, wittingly or not, however true or not, added yet another description of an Asian man in which his identity is circumscribed by femininity, especially in contrast to Western men of European descent. But the feminine qualities are not limited to the narrator's interpretation of the known facts, the description of the body. Rather, in what is meant to be a moment of empathy, when Tim imagines the life of the young man, even the profession he imagines has female overtones. Tim speculates that the man was a scholar. He was frightened by war. He was frightened by the responsibilities expected of men.

Naturally, then, it is Azar who is the first to comment, in his distinct and distancing way: "Oh, man, you fuckin' trashed the fucker ... You scrambled his sorry self, look at that, you *did*, you laid him out like Shredded fuckin' Wheat." Kiowa then makes Azar leave the scene, and he begins talking to Tim. The scene is an echo of one from the first episode, "The Things They Carried," wherein Kiowa wants to talk about the death of Lavender, but Norman Bowker doesn't want to hear it, until too late, when he finally demands that Kiowa talk. By that point, Kiowa no longer wants to talk. In this case, Tim never does talk, and Kiowa proceeds with conversation as if arguing with Tim, as if his persuasion worked against Tim's non-existent responses.

Tim continues to imagine the life of the young man. He notices such details as butterflies and blue flowers surrounding the disfigured corpse. The characteristics of the corpse's face begin to take on significance and abstraction as well. The wound at the eye, in particular, is star-shaped. There is also movement, of a sort, as the blood continues to flow from his neck, and pollen dances above him in the air. The imagery is a mix of death and ruin with beauty and movement. Even the life Tim imagined had movement, resonant with the image of the eye wound: "His life was now a constellation of possibilities."

As Tim's thoughts vacillate between the death and the state of the body and the possible lives it led, Kiowa continues the rationalization, as well as his entreaties for Tim to talk. Tim does not talk, and yet he is also the teller of the story. In the same way, the young man he has killed is no more, but, Tim imagines, just before he died, the young man "knew he would fall dead and wake up in the stories of his village and people." In the last episode of the book, O'Brien writes, "stories save us." In this instance, the story is the conversation Kiowa calls for, and it is the afterlife of the young man. There are implications later that both individuals are saved by Tim's retelling of this story, but one is also acutely aware of how easy it is for the living to say so.

Ambush

While "The Man I Killed" is the story of Tim's imagining the life of the young man through narration of the action after the death, "Ambush" is an imagined confession, an apologia for Tim's actions. The piece also acts as though the events of the book are true, and of the author.

Tim's daughter ostensibly prompts "Ambush" when she asks Tim if he had ever killed anyone. Incidentally, her asking itself could be considered an "ambush," as it represents the way the war can suddenly come back in force into the character's life.

She asks when she is nine, old enough to understand intellectually the necessity of killing while perhaps too young to empathize with or understand the complicated emotions brought out in her father when considering his deeds. As a result, his reaction, in spite of her ability to figure out that he *must* have killed someone, is to lie. He says, "Of course not," then holds her on his lap. He *wants* to tell her the truth, "exactly what happened, or what I remember happening."

The statement stands as a hinge between the episode before and the one to follow. In "The Man I Killed," there is no contemplative monologue, whereas in "Ambush," Tim is able to walk the reader through what he thinks he remembers. But the walk-through is as much for the benefit of the narrator as it is for the reader, or the one-day grown-up daughter. The process of telling, of remembering all the considerations that passed through his head in the seconds during which he considered whether to kill the man, is a form of penance, a kind of suffering and consideration that is the cost of living through such actions. His desire to know and, in effect, perhaps change or rationalize, or at least seek absolution through confession is, as he writes, "why I keep writing war stories."

After thorough, evocative description of the pain, nausea, and fear that dogged his decision to kill the man, Tim admits the nature of the moment: "It was not a matter of live or die. There was no real peril. Almost certainly the young man would have passed by. And it will always be that way."

As a grunt infantry soldier deep in the jungles of Vietnam, it is almost inconceivable that Tim did not kill other men besides the slender scholar. However, his memory is fastened on this one kill perhaps because of its needlessness. In a book that considers the needlessness of the war itself, the inclusion of this death can tempt readers to consider it a metaphor. Such a consideration could be extremely off the mark from the perspective of the book's narrator, given his thoughts on what constitutes a "true" war story. But the piece's tempting construction is perhaps also a meaningful inclusion because of how it quickens the constancy of needlessness into a focused moment in the book. The moral plight of this character who cannot undo the needlessness is one of the legacies of the war for many, many men and women. As Tim writes, "Even now I haven't finished sorting it out." Hence, the collection of episodes, and, later in the book, the trip back to Vietnam, to the shit field site of Kiowa's death, and the constancy of conflict the character lives with forever. In fact, as Tim writes in the last paragraph, the images and trauma of the war can "ambush" those who lived through it, "out of the morning fog." Out of the dawn of something new, it all returns, regardless of how he may try not to dwell on it.

Speaking of Courage

"Speaking of Courage" stands out from other episodes in *The Things They Carried* because the third-person limited narrative perspective stays very close to Norman Bowker, rather than to Tim, as it does for the majority of the other stories. The only other pieces to use a similar perspective are "The Things They Carried" and "In the Field," both of which stay somewhat close to Jimmy Cross's perspective.

"Speaking of Courage" also stands out because the action of the story takes place so long after the war. Driving his father's big Chevy, with air conditioning and radio both blasting, Norman Bowker is following a tar road around the lake in is hometown in Minnesota on the Fourth of July. At the time the story begins, Bowker has already been around the large lake six times. As he does so, he reflects on the place, on its beauty and serenity, on the houses with their gardeners, on the fate of all those he knew in high school who have moved on, the majority of whom did not go to the war.

Norman Bowker wants to talk, more than anything. But as he circles the lake, it becomes ever clearer how there is no one to talk to. Sally Kramer, now Gustafson, is a woman whose pictures Bowker used to carry in his wallet. Now, she is married, and happy, and, he imagines, would not want to hear about the war. As he drives, he also wonders what his father might say, were he there in the Chevy. But, he is not. A veteran himself (he "had his own war and ... now preferred silence"), he is at home, watching baseball. Sally, Max, and his father comprise those left in America who do not know the war. Sally is a housewife who wants to keep focused on her life. Bowker almost slows down to talk to her as he sees her, but then accelerates as he passes by, realizing, "there was really nothing he could say to her." His father is a baseball fan, and not much more. He is watching the game, Bowker says, "on national TV." And Max is dead, an ear infection keeping him from war, adulthood, and the maturity that brings with it a deadening of enthusiasm for ideas. Bowker imagines conversations about the war with all of them, conversations he will never have, and which will haunt him. The first time he thinks of his father watching baseball, he merely shrugs to himself. "'No problem,' he murmured."

He imagines telling Sally how he can now tell time without clocks, and that if he starts a conversation that way, he might get to telling her about how he almost won the Silver Star for valor. He suspects she wouldn't understand, and they wouldn't get to it anyway. He reiterates his need to talk: "If Sally had not been married, or if his father were not such a baseball fan, it would have been a good time to talk."

The talking here resonates with the several instances in the book when one soldier urges another to talk, and no real talk then occurs. Or, if there is dialogue, it is ironic, as in the case of the men talking about Lavender's "mellow" war, or singing "Lemon Tree" when cleaning up Curt Lemon's scattered body parts. Bowker is, readers learn later, the extreme result of the inability to process. He kills himself for lack of being able to talk.

Bowker imagines telling his father the story of the shit field. As he does, he explains the meaninglessness of his medals ("They were for common valor. The routine, the daily stuff— just humping, just enduring—but that was worth something, wasn't it?"), and how when faced with the opportunity to act with uncommon valor, he simply couldn't handle the stink of the fields. While imagining the conversation, he imagines he is in a tour bus, seeing the park and the high school and all the houses:

He drove slowly. No hurry, nowhere to go. Inside the Chevy the air was cool and oily-smelling, and he took pleasure in the steady sounds of the engine and air conditioning. A tour bus feeling, in a way, except the town he was touring seemed dead. Through the windows, as if in a stop motion photograph, the place looked as if it had been hit by nerve gas, everything still and lifeless, even the people. The town could not talk, and would not listen. "How'd you like to hear about the war?" he might have asked, but the place could only blink and shrug. It had no memory, therefore no guilt. The taxes got paid and the votes got counted and the agencies of government did their work briskly and politely. It was a brisk, polite town. It did not know shit about shit, and did not care to know.

Norman Bowker leaned back and considered what he might've said on the subject. He knew shit. It was his specialty. The smell, in particular, but also the numerous varieties or texture and taste. Someday he'd give a lecture on the topic. Put on a suit and tie up in front of the Kiwanis club and tell the fuckers about all the wonderful shit he knew. Pass out samples, maybe.

Though Bowker smiles at what he imagines, the scene is bitter, angry, dejected. As he continues to imagine the horror of the camp and telling about it to his father, he keeps imagining, too, what Sally or Max would think. With Sally, he imagines her objecting to the use of the word "shit." He replies, "That's what it *was*." What he endured can only be described in words no one who is "polite" wants to hear. He does not want his experiences dismissed or buried because the words are too much for some, since the words pale, obviously, next to the experience itself. For Bowker, if they refuse the words, do they then refuse him at a deeper level?

After realizing "this was not a story for Sally Kramer," Bowker thinks of his father's reaction. "If his father were here ... [he] might have glanced over for a second, understanding perfectly well that it was not a question of offensive language but of fact. His father would have sighed and folded his arms and waited."

Bowker continues around the lake. The preparations for the night's fireworks are nearly complete. He sees the same people again and again, a man in a failing motorboat, the high school band, a woman fishing. He notes the hour, around seven, and the day's lazy ending, and he wishes someone were there to speak with him. "Still," he thinks, "there was so much to say." The urge is so powerful that the line is its own paragraph.

And so the story of the shit field goes on. After letting the mama-sans convince the group to bivouac near the river in the field, the rains come in and pound their encampment. They stayed, and Bowker tells how sometimes "the difference between courage and cowardice was something small and stupid." It is foreshadowing for the small and stupid thing that means the difference between life and death for Kiowa. The soldiers took mortar fire late in the night, and the field "was boiling" from the shelling and the rain and the chaos. In the midst of it, Kiowa sinks into the muck. "There were bubbles where Kiowa's head should have been." When Bowker tries to help him, the circumstances overwhelm, and something "small" and "stupid" keeps the man from "courage:"

> He would've talked about this, and how he grabbed Kiowa by the boot and tried to pull him out. He pulled hard but Kiowa was gone, and then suddenly felt himself going too. He could taste it. The shit was in his nose and eyes. There were flares and mortar rounds, and the stink was everywhere—it was inside him, in his lungs—and he could no longer tolerate it. Not here, he thought. Not like this. He released Kiowa's boot and watched it slide away. Slowly, working his way up, he hoisted himself out of the deep mud, and then he lay still and tasted the shit in his mouth and closed his eyes and listened to the rain and explosions and bubbling sounds.
>
> He was alone.
>
> He had lost his weapon but it did not matter. All he wanted was a bath.

Nothing else. A hot soapy bath.

Circling the lake, Norman Bowker remembered how his friend Kiowa had disappeared under the waste and water.

"I didn't flip out," he would've said. "I was cool. If things had gone right, if it hadn't been for that smell, I could've won the Silver Star."

A good war story, he thought, but it was not a war for war stories, nor for talk of valor, and nobody in town wanted to know about the terrible stink. They wanted good intentions and good deeds. But the town was not to blame, really. It was a nice little town, very prosperous, with neat houses and all the sanitary conveniences.

He decides to pull in to the A&W stand to get a bite before the fireworks. He talks to the intercom for his order, and when the voice tells him he'd listen to a story, Bowker declines. He eats, and returns to his revolutions. People are headed indoors, he finds, and the evening has cooled to the point where he rolls down the windows. After being given a chance to talk and declining it, he then comes to the conclusion, on revolution number eleven, "There was nothing to say. He could not talk about it and never would ... He wished he could've explained some of this. How he had been braver than he ever thought possible, but how he had not been so brave as he wanted to be."

Notes

In "Notes," the narrator and ostensible composer of "Speaking of Courage" comes clean: Tim is the one who failed to save Kiowa from the shit field. The story takes its title from the literary tradition of explanatory notes meant to illuminate sources and strategies within a piece. While this piece does clarify things, it also reveals "Speaking of Courage" to be Tim's—the narrator's—attempt to deflect the reality of Kiowa's death onto someone else.

As the note says, the story was written at Bowker's suggestion, in 1975. Readers also learn, right away, that Bowker killed himself three years afterward. Up until the end of the story, one might assume that guilt over Kiowa led him to it, except that Tim reveals that Bowker had nothing to do with Kiowa's death. The revelation underscores, once again, how it is unwise to trust such causal formulae in O'Brien's collection.

Readers learn Bowker's seventeen page letter to the narrator inspires the story. The letter is Bowker's means of finally "talking" about the war. He tells Tim how he went through several jobs, lived with his parents, stayed in bed a lot—exhibiting classic behaviors associated with depression. The letter moves over several emotions, and Bowker repeatedly upbraids himself for complaining. Finally, Bowker gets to the reason he wrote: he had read O'Brien's first book, *If I Die in a Combat Zone*, liked it, and thought he had a good story idea. He tells Tim he needs to write about a "guy who can't get his act together and just drives around town all day and can't think of any damn place to go and doesn't know how to get there anyway. The guy wants to talk about it, but he *can't* ... If you want, you can use the stuff in this letter."

Tim says, "Bowker's letter hit me hard." He meditates on his own ability to have successfully rejoined society, even though he admits he has written the story several times, as catharsis, communication, or simply assertion of the reality of something no one wanted to talk about much in the 1970s. As he does so, he drifts into philosophizing about truth again:

> ... it occurred to me that the act of writing had led me through a swirl of memories that might otherwise have ended in paralysis or worse. By telling stories, you objectify your own experience. You separate it from yourself. You pin down certain truths. You make up others. You start sometimes with an incident that truly happened, like the night in the shit field, and you carry it forward by inventing incidents that did not in fact occur but that nonetheless help to clarify and explain.

Tim then talks about the story's first shape. It was written during the time the "author" was also composing *Going After*

Cacciato, and since it was a post-war story, as opposed to a war story, Tim published it on its own. However, he points out, "Almost immediately, though, there was a sense of failure. The details of Norman Bowker's story were missing." Tim tells how the novel's particulars had forced him to leave out the shit field, the rain and shelling, and Kiowa. This could be a lie on the narrator's part. At the end of the story, he admits that those elements were not, in fact, part of Bowker's experience—or, at least, not as Tim imagines them. Bowker had been in the shit field, but the experience for Bowker was not nearly as fraught as it was for Tim, simply because Bowker did not, in fact, allow Kiowa to die. Thus, when Tim writes, "What that piece needed, and did not have, was the terrible killing power of that shit field," the killing power he imagines is not just what killed Kiowa, but what prevented Tim from doing more to save him, a feeling Bowker could not have had. What is omitted then is not Bowker's story, but parts of Tim's that make him feel its power. As he says, "something about the story had frightened me—I was afraid to speak directly, afraid to remember—and in the end the piece had been ruined by a failure to tell the full and exact truth about our night in the shit field." Tim's fear is one borne of guilt and a shame he had not yet dealt with.

Still, according to the story, when Tim sends Bowker the anthology with the story reprinted, Bowker reminds him of what was missing: "You left out Vietnam. Where's Kiowa? Where's the shit?" Eight months afterward, Bowker kills himself, and leaves no note or other clue as to why. However, Tim positions the news of the death immediately after Bowker's pointing out the failure of the story, as if Tim was Bowker's last hope at true talk and, having failed him, left him no choice. The implication is that some of the other things Tim now carries are the lives of two of his fellow soldiers.

In the Field

After the night in the shit field, the soldiers begin the task of locating Kiowa's remains. This episode returns to the narrative perspective of the first episode, "The Things They Carried," and thus is the only other story in the book to be told in anything resembling an omniscient viewpoint. In this case, the third-person omniscient viewpoint is limited to the perspective of Jimmy Cross, but it still maintains a distance from the actual events, thus allowing the narration to articulate thoughts Cross might, in the stress of the moment, be unable to formulate.

However, the distant narration also serves as another veneer for truth and the actual. Distance, to many readers, translates as objectivity. Because this is not "Tim" telling the story, or any of the others—Rat Kiley, Mitchell Saunders, and so on— retelling a tale (as in "Sweetheart of the Song Tra Bong"), "In the Field" comes across as more "true." That sense of verisimilitude is further heightened by the seemingly objective narration telling a story that has been referred to throughout the book. The effect is one of the reader coming to the story, hearing the voice, and settling in to hear, now, finally, what *really* happened. But the wary reader, the one who has been paying attention during some episodes, chiefly "How To Tell A True War Story," knows that the book depends on the gut feeling of truth, taking its horrific power *from* the actual, even if the tales themselves are fiction.

Since readers know that Tim was the one who let Kiowa slip under the mud, and that he blames himself for it, they will recognize the boy Jimmy Cross encounters first in the episode: "The young soldier stood off by himself in the center of the field in knee-deep water, reaching down with both hands as if chasing some object just beneath the surface. The boy's shoulders were shaking. Jimmy Cross yelled but the young soldier did not turn or look up." Cross considers his mistake in camping in the shit field, and begins to think about his blame for the death. He acknowledges he could have flouted orders, or at least suggested to the high-ups that the site was unsuitable, but he didn't. Then, his thoughts turn to the letter he wants to write to Kiowa's parents, to let them know "what a fine human being" their son had been.

Meanwhile, Azar makes jokes about dying in shit, annoying both Norman Bowker and Mitchell Sanders. As they look for Kiowa, they turn up his rucksack, with the moccasins and the

New Testament. When Bowker suggests they tell Cross, Sanders says, "Screw him." Sanders blames Cross for the mistake of the camp, despite Bowker's attempts to suggest the situation was blameless. The balance of the story is the meditation on blame. The shit field itself is a metaphor, read literally and read as all of Vietnam. At the same time, the men's arguing over fault regarding the death of Kiowa is an argument over the blame for Vietnam. Each individual in the shit field feels he knows who is to blame—himself, others, all of them, none of them, the higher-ups, and so on. Each also suspects it is beyond them. Just as Tim's reverie in Burdahl's boat included things he could not possibly know, the circular meditation on blame includes so many steps the men can't know.

Cross approaches the question of blame through the letter and its gradual composition. The thought of it keeps him serene during the arduous search. On the other hand, the young soldier transfers his grief into frustration at his lost photograph. Readers know he will later revisit the shit field throughout his life, but at the moment he is assuaging his own sense of guilt by enumerating the number of causes related to his own action. The photo itself has to be found because of its role in the death; he had turned on a flashlight briefly so Kiowa might see his girlfriend, at which point their location was given away, and the field "exploded all around them." He lost Kiowa in the confusion, as well as the photo, the flashlight, "everything." In the shit field, he remembers all he lost, and he "remembered wondering if he could lose himself."

Jimmy Cross knows none of it, and so does not understand the rationale behind the boy's fevered search for a photograph. As he watches him, he pities the boy. He has no idea of the depth of the boy's own reasons and blame. He sees the boy's actions as hopeless, working "as if something might be salvaged from all the waste." In saying so, he characterizes implicitly the actions of all the men in the shit field, and in Vietnam, as inherently futile.

Finally, when Azar, Sanders, and Bowker find Kiowa's body and unearth it, Azar is the one most clearly shaken up. For all his joking and machismo, he is the one clutching his guts and "pale." After they clean the body, the narration shifts into a moment of pure omniscience:

> For all of them it was a relief to have it finished. There was the promise now of finding a hootch somewhere, or an abandoned pagoda, where they could strip down and wring out their fatigues and maybe start a hot fire. They felt bad for Kiowa. But they also felt a kind of giddiness, a secret joy, because they were alive, and because even the rain was preferable to being sucked under a shit field, and because it was all a matter of luck and happenstance.

Not only are they happy, secretly and momentarily, their suspicion that it all amounted to luck and happenstance effectively mutes the matter of blame and consequence. Does fault matter in the face of randomness? Finally, however, Azar comes to Bowker, chastened by finding the body, and apologizes for the joking, saying that he feels guilty, as if nothing would have happened if he'd kept his mouth shut. Bowker doesn't look at him, and says, as if to everyone, "'Nobody's fault,' he said. 'Everybody's.'"

In the final section of the episode, the boy soldier is still looking for the photograph, and by now wants to confess to his lieutenant that his flashlight and the photo had led to the attack which killed Kiowa. As he goes to explain, Cross has already tuned him out. Cross has fallen into the field, and is floating on the shit. As he does, he goes through a list of all the ways anyone could assign the blame for Kiowa's death and for Vietnam. As he fantasizes himself back home, he realizes he may or may not ever write the letter to Kiowa's death, because what *would* he say? If you can blame everyone, what is the cause? He thinks, "When a man died, there had to be blame." Yet, when none of the blame makes sense or holds, or it all does, is there any immediacy? He says that, in the field, "the causes were immediate. A moment of carelessness or bad judgment or plain stupidity carried consequences that lasted forever." But the field, as has already been established in many episodes of *The Things they Carried*, is simply not translatable to a world of everyday experience. Blame, thus, is similarly burdened.

Good Form; Field Trip

By the time most readers get to "Good Form," they have learned not to trust O'Brien in the ways one would trust a conventional narrator. When he writes, "It's time to be blunt," it's almost a guarantee he is *not* being blunt. He says he is a writer, that he is forty-three, and that "a long time ago I walked through Quang Ngai Province as a foot soldier." Then, he tells us "Almost everything else is invented."

He then tells a story of the man killed on a path near My Khe, tells of his "burden of responsibility and grief" simply because he was there, a burden not unlike the one groped for by the men in the shit field. Yet, then he says, "Even *that* story is made up." A few paragraphs later, though, he reiterates the details from the story—the star-shaped hole, the daintiness of the man—and insists, "I killed him." The piece's resistance to settle on a definitive statement of fact is part of O'Brien's larger meditation on truth and blame.

He says, in one of the most quoted lines from the entire book: "I want you to feel what I felt. I want you to know why story-truth is truer sometimes than happening-truth." His larger point, perhaps, is that as much as he was there, alive, taking part, he was a part of the atrocities committed. Whether he sanctioned them at the time—or later, or before, or not—is irrelevant. That he felt, experienced, and is fighting to deal with the truth, however troublesome and elusive it may be, is all. It is important that this admission, this show of "good form" comes after a story wherein blame is both everywhere and nowhere, wherein men search for a body, reasons, artifacts, and blame in a field of bombed out waste. It is further important that the narrator speaking directly to the reader is nearly irrelevant, and not as much of an impact as the bluntness of the episodes themselves.

When he says stories can "make things present," he refers to fiction writers' skill of inventing details to cultivate in the reader a belief in both the actuality and the immediacy of the story. Edgar Allen Poe once claimed that readers enter a story with a willing suspension of disbelief. But O'Brien acknowledges that writers bear the burden of cultivating a sense of belief in the reader, and such cultivation does not depend on the actuality of a thing's happening or being. Rather, it depends on the impact of the details and their degree of verisimilitude. And for the writer/soldier, as O'Brien says, "I can look at things I never looked at. I can attach faces to grief and love and pity and God. I can be brave. I can make myself feel again." The writer, in this case, can give substance to the inchoate; in short, he can do the work of metaphor.

At the end of the short piece, the daughter, Kathleen, is again invoked. When he imagines her demanding the truth of whether or not he killed anyone, he realizes he has two answers, yes and no, depending on his interpretation of truth and blame. With such semantics playing a central role in the life of the ostensible narrator, the veracity of the entire book is questioned. But does it matter? If the book remains as powerful as virtually every critic has asserted, and as millions of readers have found as well, does veracity matter? Does the fact that the book asks such a question matter?

In "Field Trip," all such questions are shunted aside again so that the story can pick up with the development of the narrator, Tim. After writing "In the Field," which readers have just been told is not true, the writer tells readers that after completing the story, he went back to the site of Kiowa's death, taking his daughter with him. He says, simply, "The place was at peace." In fact, farmers in the now bucolic setting look up once at him, quizzically, and then return to their work.

He has not told his daughter why they are there. When she goes to stand by him as he snaps pictures, she announces that it "stinks." She wants to say more, but doesn't. Readers already know she finds her father weird, as most ten-year-old girls do, but her comment is also one she suspects her father has an answer for. But he doesn't. She keeps asking him questions, and he keeps disappointing her with answers that, to him, are as honest as he can be without lengthy explanations, but that to her are non-answers.

"This whole war," she said, "why was everybody so mad at everybody else?"

I shook my head. "They weren't mad, exactly. Some people wanted one thing, other people wanted another thing."

"What did *you* want?"

"Nothing," I said. "To stay alive."

"That's all?"

"Yes."

Kathleen sighed. "Well, I don't get it. I mean, how come you were even here in the first place?"

"I don't know," I said. "Because I had to be."

"But *why*?"

I tried to find something to tell her, but finally I shrugged and said, "It's a mystery, I guess. I don't know."

He had wanted to take her to Quang Ngai, to "the Vietnam that kept me awake at night," hoping to revisit the trail outside My Khe, where he had killed the thin man. With time running out for their stay, however, and having to hit certain landmarks for his daughter, he opted instead for the site of the shit field. Seeing the field that had grown past its desctruction some twenty years before, Tim "wondered if it was all a mistake. Everything was too ordinary. A quiet sunny day, and the field was not the field I remembered." Tim's experience is similar, to some ways, of Norman Bowker's returning to his small town to find it menacingly the same but altered. The field, just like Bowker's town, is a disappointment:

After that long night in the rain, I'd seemed to grow cold inside, all the illusions gone, all the old ambitions and hopes for myself sucked away into the mud. Over the years, that coldness had never entirely disappeared. There were times in my life when I couldn't feel much, not sadness or pity or passion, and I blamed it for taking away the person I had once been. For twenty years this field had embodied all the waste that was Vietnam, all the vulgarity and horror.

Now, it was just what it was. Flat and dreary and unremarkable.

In this way, the narrator reveals the field as a thing of his making. The very thing no longer exists. To bring it back, to make readers understand it, takes the power of story. Fiction can render it not only as it must be for the sake of the story, but can create it as something other, something different from the original or what is left behind, so that the timeless creation of the story is something that, like the field in Tim's mind, can haunt and haunt again.

Once Tim realizes how the field has changed, he decides to place Kiowa's rucksack back into the field, having taken it with him, it seems, expressly for that purpose. He walks past where Jimmy Cross had set up his post, and tries to stand approximately where Mitchell Saunders had found the rucksack. He wedges the moccasins into the mud. He had done what he had wanted to do for Kiowa, but found that after the gesture, "I tried to think of something decent to say, something meaningful and right, but nothing came to me." Just as the field had changed, so had the items, the gesture, the memory of Kiowa itself.

He exchanges glances with one of the old men, who looks at him with some hostility. When he walks back across the field with Kathleen, after the hollow gesture, she says that the man looked mad. He says, "No ... All that's finished." However, as readers understand from reading about this man, it is not over. And as readers also understand from the guidelines set forth by "How To Tell A True War Story," the conflict, in all its permutation, is also not over, especially for Tim.

The Ghost Soldiers; Night Life

Together, the episodes detail the dissolution, for Tim, of Alpha Company. "The Ghost Soldiers" is among the more complicated pieces of *The Things They Carried*, as it covers Tim's separation from Alpha Company, the experience of revenge and "becoming one" with the experience of the war, the moral codes of the men, and the departure of Rat Kiley.

The episode starts with Tim telling of the two times he was shot. He tells of both times to show the difference between the experienced, almost light care of Rat Kiley and the ineptitude of Bobby Jorgenson. Even their names—Rat, Bobby—suggest the fundamental difference between the two.

The first time Tim is shot, he bounces off the wall of a pagoda and lands in Rat's lap. Rat's care is expert, swift, and funny. He says to Tim, "just a side wound, no problem unless you're pregnant." He leaves to help two others who have fallen, saying "Happy trails" before heading into fire. Just as Tim is loaded into the chopper to head for R&R, Rat "did an odd thing. He leaned in and put his head against my shoulder and almost hugged me. Coming from Rat Kiley, that was something new."

Tim is only away for twenty-six days. The wound is treated quickly, there is no infection, it heals well. It is, in fact, exactly the opposite of what happens with Jorgenson. Tim meets Bobby when he returns from recovery, and immediately he notices that "Jorgenson was no Rat Kiley ... he was green and incompetent and scared." When Tim is shot in the buttocks, Jorgenson watches it happens, and fear seizes him. He is unable to act:

> ... when I got shot the second time, in the butt, along the Song Tra Bong, it took the son of a bitch almost ten minutes to work up the nerve to crawl over to me. By then I was gone with the pain. Later I found out I almost died of shock. Bobby Jorgenson didn't know about the shock, or if he did, fear made him forget. To make matters worse, he bungled the patch job, and a couple of weeks later my ass started to rot away. You could actually pull big chunks off with your fingernail.
>
> It was borderline gangrene. I spent a month flat on my stomach; I couldn't walk or sit; I couldn't sleep. I kept

seeing Bobby Jorgenson's scared-white face. Those buggy eyes and the way his lips twitched and that silly excuse he had for a mustache. After the rot cleared up, once I could think straight, I devoted a lot of time to figuring ways to get back at him.

Tim has to rub ointment on the wound, three times a day, to prevent any further rot. For Tim, it is the height of indignity. The ordeal is made worse by how the nurses mock him. The "recovery" made him feel robbed of the ability to salvage the one thing worth salvaging from such an experience: the ability to tell it. If one lives through trauma, he reasons, you should have the right to tell it without embarrassment. In his logic, Jorgenson not only nearly killed him and forced him to recover from a horrible injury and its botched aftermath, but he robbed him of the story he could have told. Thus readers see again the power of story, and the place it has in the book's ideas of importance.

But for Tim, the toll of Jorgenson's ineptitude is not complete until after "the higher-ups decided [he]'d been shot enough." He is transferred to S-4, the battalion supply station, a place as safe, Tim assures us, as a baseball stadium in Minnesota. He is immersed in "the whole blurry slow motion of the rear." He is away from the fighting, and he began to miss the "adventure, even the danger, of the real war out in the boonies. It's a hard thing to explain to somebody who hasn't felt it, but the presence of death and danger has a way of bringing you fully awake ... You become part of a tribe and you share the same blood." The injury has not only taken him out of the war, its prolonged nature has removed him from the fraternity of men who "get it." In some ways, he ceases to be a soldier. Just as Mary Anne seemed to look down on Fossie in "Sweetheart of the Song Tra Bong," and just as Bowker could not explain the war to Sally Gustafson, and just as so many other soldiers had moments when what they experienced could not be translated to someone who wasn't there, Tim experiences the change from one who was there to one who, now, is not.

Tim realizes his change in status when Alpha Company comes in to S-4 for "stand-down." The group parties and tells stories and as they start, Tim looks at Norman Bowker and has the realization:

> In a way, I envied him—all of them. Their deep brush tans, the sores and blisters, the stories, the in-it-togetherness. I felt close to them, yes, but I also felt a new degree of separation. My fatigues were starched; I had a neat haircut and the clean, sterile smell of the rear. They were still my buddies, on one level, but once you leave the boonies, the whole comrade business gets turned around. You become a civilian.

The realization is finally expressed when Mitchell Sanders tells Tim, directly, that Jorgenson is "*with* us now" and "I guess you're not." Thus, when Tim finally runs into Jorgenson, his feelings are at their worst, and while Jorgenson tries to apologize, Tim doesn't let him. He feels bad for Jorgenson's position, and understands, intellectually, that the man had gotten better at the work since then, and he had earned the respect of Tim's former brothers-in-arms. But the other result of the meeting is that Tim finds another reason to hate him: "I hated him for making me stop hating him."

After ruminating on how changed he has become, how a "quiet, thoughtful" Phi Beta Kappa and summa cum laude college grad from the Midwest had "somehow been crushed under the weight of daily realities," Tim decides to enlist Azar in a scheme to get revenge on Jorgenson. He picks Azar for a lot of reasons. Azar had a cruel sense of justice, few loyalties, was not well-liked by anyone else and so felt no compunction about dealing with Jorgenson, and because Sanders wouldn't help him. Sanders dismisses him as "sick." Tim is thus alienated in another way.

The plan is to make Jorgenson think he is under attack. To execute the plan, Azar and Tim have to rig ordinance and other "ghost" props in the jungle in front of the post where Jorgenson will sit night watch. As they begin, Azar characterizes Jorgenson as a "roast pigeon on a spit," a sitting duck. Tim says, "Except this isn't for real," but Azar shrugs. Azar still loves the thrill of the war, the feel of combat, and while some of the deaths have bothered him, the moment gives him a rush. Tim begins to sense that he was mistaken to have involved Azar, as Azar would make the gag much more real and terrifying than Tim wanted it to be.

For all that Tim claims to have changed, he is not an extreme person like Azar. There are still gradations in the story: Tim is not Mary Anne, not Azar, not repressive like Bowker, and neither is he pure like Kiowa, nor timid and pacific like Lavender. While there is a brutish lumping of type and comrade in many aspects of the war experience for Tim and the others, Tim's struggles reveal points of separateness. Just as the things they carried are categorized, the characters are also moved, toward the end of the book, into separate spheres, re-humanized, so to speak. The struggle of this penultimate episode is that Tim has reached his limit, has realized his capacity for cruelty, and is furiously trying to back away from the precipice he sees in Azar. But he also cannot extricate himself from the events and still save face, still have a chance of rejoining the fraternity to which he no longer belongs.

He is denied a graceful exit the entire way. They decide to run the prank at night, knowing it is the time when men are most scared. As they run through its steps, and begin to spook Jorgenson, Tim is surprised at the "swell of immense power" he feels while watching Jorgenson play into the prank.

It was a feeling the VC must have. Like a puppeteer. Yank on the ropes, watch the silly wooden soldier jump and twitch. It made me smile ...

In a way, I wanted to stop myself. It was cruel, I knew that, but right and wrong were somewhere else. This was the spirit world.

I heard myself laugh.

In order to accomplish such cruelty, he has to become the "other," the enemy. He wants his morality to keep him from doing such a thing, but it won't. So he invents something which takes his place. In a final moment of leaving himself, he imagines himself in the bunker with Jorgenson, and the final metamorphosis takes place:

> I was down there with him, inside him. I was part of the night. I was the land itself—everything, everywhere—the fireflies and paddies, the moon, the midnight rustlings, the cool phosphorescent shimmer of evil—I was atrocity—I was jungle fire, jungle drums—I was the blind stare in the eye of all those poor, dead, dumbfuck ex-pals of mine—all the pale young corpses, Lee Strunk and Kiowa and Curt Lemon—I was the beast on their lips—I was Nam—the horror, the war.

The transformation is the closest he comes to being someone like Mary Anne or the Greenies. It scares him. As the prank unfolds, and he hears Jorgenson make "a short lung-and-throat bark" of fear, Tim says, "There ... now you know." Tim wanted to make the other man feel fear, and he thinks he has heard evidence of it. He thinks, "You know you're about to die. And it's not a movie and you aren't a hero and all you can do is whimper and wait. This, now, was something we shared."

He feels close, more than compassion, as if he and Jorgenson are now kindred spirits, both having been outsiders, both having been terrified by the war. His identifying with Jorgenson makes him finally tell Azar that the prank is over. Azar ignores him, and relishes the discomfort it causes Tim, and the panic that builds in Jorgenson. As Azar continues, Tim remembers again the moment he was shot, and how he yelled to Jorgenson, then for him to treat for shock. Recalling how he felt as if his spirit left his body, he compares it to the feeling overcoming him as he waits for morning, and the end of what is now Azar's prank. Tim continues to beg Azar to stop, and eventually Jorgenson goes out to confront the soldier he thinks is on the perimeter, and he discovers the gag.

Tim is trembling, crouched, fearful, and Azar regards him with contempt. Before leaving, he kicks Tim in the head. Jorgenson treats the wound, and the men decide that they are even. They don't shake hands. They do not say anything meaningful. Tim even jokes about getting Azar. He delivers the joke in such a way that, after the accumulation of episodes and the reader's realization that there are really no jokes that don't have layers of meaning in the context of *The Things They Carried*, Tim's offhand suggestion to kill Azar is not funny. Nor is it meaningful. The urge for death and vengeance is thus reduced to a nothing statement, a null.

As for Rat Kiley, "Night Life" reveals that Rat left Alpha Company by shooting himself in the foot, unable and unwilling to endure the erosion of night patrol, the fear, and the hallucinatory visions that came to him.

The Lives of the Dead

The last episode of the book is also its *ars poetica*. In it, Tim describes the source of his method for what Bobbie Ann Mason terms "deflective techniques." He starts out with the assertion, "But this too is true: stories can save us." Hence, the impetus for putting the stories to paper. As is implied throughout the more meditative, direct-address episodes of the book, Tim is trying to save the men of Alpha Company, the people they knew and who knew him, and even, especially, himself. He keeps "dreaming Linda alive. And Ted Lavender, too, and Kiowa, and Curt Lemon" and many more, their names sung again and again, gaining the repetition of incantation or prayer.

He gives a first example, "a body without a name" which the men of Alpha Company have found and are greeting. Each soldier walks up to the body, greets it, and shakes the hand of the dead man. Tim, still new to the war, "it was my fourth day," is sickened physically by the sight. Dave Jensen suggests that it is "too real" and Tim concurs. Later, when they toast the corpse, Tim can't take part in that gesture either. Only Kiowa tells him he was good to avoid doing it. When Tim tells Kiowa that the man reminds him of a girl he took to the movies once,

Kiowa, not understanding that Tim isn't joking, tells him "that's a bad date."

But Linda, readers learn, is a young girl who eventually died of a brain tumor. Tim recalls how he loved her, despite their age: "it's tempting to dismiss it as a crush, an infatuation of childhood, but I know for a fact that what we felt for each other was a s deep and rich as love can ever get." Tim admired her bearing and her grace, as he saw it, and on their first date, he yearned to articulate all the things he felt, wanted to tell her "big profound things," but struggled. In the end, he complemented the long red cap she wore on her head. It was a minor compliment that both children knew was sincere, but for which his mother shot him a "hard look." In the theater, they can not talk to one another, but again, Tim insists that inability was due to the understood emotions between them.

Tim then pauses the Linda story to interject once again, musing on the nature of storytelling. He says, "The thing about a story is that you dream it as you tell it, hoping that others might then dream along with you, and in this way memory and imagination and language combine to make spirits in the head." This reference comes after the spirit world evoked in "The Ghost Soldiers," after the ghosts and spirits of "Sweetheart of the Song Tra Bong," of the shit field, and more. The ghost world imagined is, he implies, accessible only through story. If the Vietnam experience thus was ghost-like, or was complete only on understanding the plane that the men could not articulate to "civilians" and others, then stories were the only other way to access it short of being in country.

The men themselves participated in stories to keep death at bay. Tim tells, once again, of the time Lavender was shot. Only in this version, readers learn a detail not told the first time. After they had stripped him of his effects and equipment and covered him with a poncho, Mitchell Sanders asked the body, "Hey Lavender ... how's the war today?" Somebody eventually answered, "Mellow." They tell Lavender of the chopper ride to come, then, and how it will be mellow. Then, "We could almost see Ted Lavender's dreamy blue eyes. We could almost hear him." The other sounds they hear, the wind and birds, are merely "the world we were in." Then, Tim tells the reader:

That's what a story does. The bodies are animated, You make the dead talk. They sometimes say things like, "Roger that." Or they say, "Timmy, stop crying," which is what Linda said to me after she was dead.

At that point, Tim returns to the Linda story. The movie they saw, *The Man Who Never Was*, featured a corpse, a soldier, as part of a British plot to mislead the Germans about a beach landing. The movie and its corpse stand out to Tim because of his worry over whether or not Linda could handle such material, but they stand out in the book as a bald contradiction of the idea that, as in the case of Lavender or the old hand-shaking man, the dead are more than "the man who never was," they are not misleading, and they are alive in stories.

The next scene concerns Linda at school. Nick Veenhoff, a boy in Tim and Linda's class, decides to pluck her hat off in class one day, and to everyone's surprise, she is bald underneath, or mostly bald. There are a few tufts of hair, enough to make the baldness seem more profound. Her head also showed the signs of recent surgery—gauze, a Band Aid, stitches. Nick "took a step backward. He was still smiling, but the smile was doing strange things." Nick's reaction to the evidence of harm and sickness is similar to that of the green soldiers' to death in other episodes of the book. Tim met her gaze, and he "had the feeling that a whole conversation was happening between us. *Well?* she was saying, and I was saying, *Sure, okay.*"

The scene establishes why Linda will die, but it also establishes the kind of person Tim likes to think he is. It's an important claim for him; after all he goes through in Vietnam, and all the ways he thinks he has failed and changed—on Burdahl's boat, on the trail by My Khe, in the shit field, with Azar against Jorgenson, and more—he is still the same essential person. And he needs the stories of his past to confirm that for him:

It's now 1990. I'm forty-three years old, which would've seemed impossible to a fourth grader, and yet when I look at photographs of myself as I was in 1956, I realize that in the important ways I haven't changed at all. I was Timmy then; now I'm Tim. But the essence remains the same. I'm not fooled by the baggy pants or the crewcut or the happy smile—I know my own eyes—and there is no doubt that the Timmy smiling at the camera is the Tim I am now. Inside the body, or beyond the body, there is something absolute and unchanging. The human life is all one thing, like a blade tracing loops on ice: a little kid, a twenty-three-year-old infantry sergeant, a middle-aged writer knowing guilt and sorrow.

And as a writer not, I want to save Linda's life. Not her body—her life.

He then remembers the day she did die, and how he dreamed her to life to deal with it. He recalls learning how she was sick, the specifics of it, and then, the day she died, Nick Veenhoff told him she "kicked the bucket." He went home, lingered by himself, and then pictured her, with her hair back, lively, playing a game in the street where she kicked around an aluminum water bucket. He imagines telling her that he was sad because she was dead. She tells him to stop crying, that "it doesn't *matter*." It was, he recalls, a way of making her seem "not quite so dead." And it was the same thing they did in Vietnam.

The dead shook hands, or they had funny names: "a VC nurse, fried by napalm, was a crispy critter. A Vietnamese baby, which lay nearby, was a roasted peanut ... We kept the dead alive with stories." They were ways of "bringing body and soul back together"—hence the story of Curt Lemon, told more elaborately each time, where he went trick-or-treating on Halloween in a village, wearing nothing but a mask and boots. They told it often, to the point where they would imagine Lemon still out there "in the dark, naked and painted up, trick-or-treating, sliding from hootch to hootch in that crazy white ghost mask. But he was dead."

The first dead person Tim ever saw was Linda. He recalls her funeral, how unreal her body appeared in the casket, as if it were a "joke." The stories preserve what might be called a soul, or a spirit, as the bodies become unrecognizable. In the scene immediately following Tim's recollection of Linda's funeral, Tim tells of the experiences he has had with bodies in Vietnam, and their distance from life, from what life feels and smells like. He recalls the pieces of Lemon, the sinking of Kiowa, but in particular, a time when he and Mitchell Sanders are cleaning up enemy dead, tossing them into a truck. The description of the bodies centers on their complete *other*-ness, on how unlike the living they are, their bloat, their smell, their bounce, their "sharp burping sounds." When Sanders speaks "his own wisdom," it is merely, profoundly, that "death sucks."

Thus, death is to be fought, avoided, cajoled, and tricked. And it is to be fought with stories, with conjuring and the power of language. After Linda died, Tim kept making himself dream of her: "I invented my own dreams. It sounds impossible, I know, but I did it." Linda would show up, and they would talk. He began going to bed earlier so that he would dream her sooner. It helped him, but he was worried and embarrassed about what people might say if anyone knew. But he persisted. In one dream, he asked her what it was like to be dead, at which point she said it was a silly question. But, after a few moments, she answers him, making it clear that when he dreams, she is not dead, because he is dreaming her alive. But, when she is,

> ... it's like being inside a book that nobody's reading."
> "A book?" I said.
> "An old one. It's up on a library shelf, so you're safe and everything, but the book hasn't been checked out for a long, long time. All you can do is wait. Just hope somebody'll pick it up and start reading."

Hence, the book. The book, *The Things They Carried*, will allow people to read the lives of Lavender, Lemon, Kiowa, Tim, Bowker, Sanders, and the rest of them. It will allow Tim to save all that he couldn't save, and to allow it all to live. The book ends with him saying as much:

> And then it becomes 1990. I'm forty-three years old, and a writer now, still dreaming Linda alive in exactly the same way. She's not the embodied Linda; she's mostly made up, with a new identity and a new name, like the man who never was. Her real name doesn't matter. She was nine years old. I loved her then and then she died. And right here, in the spell of memory and imagination, I can still see her as if through ice, as if I'm gazing into some other world, a place where there are no brain tumors and no funeral homes, where there are no bodies at all. I can see Kiowa, too, and Ted Lavender and Curt Lemon, and sometimes I can even see Timmy skating with Linda under the yellow floodlights. I'm young and happy. I'll never die. I'm skimming across the surface of my own history, moving fast, riding the melt beneath the blades, doing loops and spins, and when I take a high leap into the dark and come down thirty years later, I realize it is as Tim trying to save Timmy's life with a story.

The confluence of Linda, Minnesota, the war, Canada, the soldiers, and the idea of stories settles solidly in the last paragraph, into the dense thatch of the things that Tim carries.

Note

1. From *You've Got To Read This: Contemporary American Writers Introduce Stories that Held Them in Awe*, New York: Perennial, 2000: pp. 422–423.

CLAYTON W. LEWIS' "CHRONICLES OF WAR"

With Michael Herr (*Dispatches*) and Philip Caputo (*A Rumor of War*), Tim O'Brien is regarded as one of the best writers to emerge from the veterans of the Vietnam war. *The Things They Carried* is a hybrid mingling of war memoir and hi-tech metafiction. The prose, ringing of wonder as well as savvy, has the dense texture of memoir and some of the urgent purpose found in Sledge and Norman. But O'Brien is also an artificer, a smart metafictionist; the narrative shapes of gorges, Barth, and Marquez make for a unique memoir.

In "The Man I Killed" O'Brien presents a lucid, guilt-ridden memory of killing at close range a single Viet Cong soldier. In the next section, "Ambush," he tells his gullible reader that he shot no one—that he was only a witness. The event we just observed dissolves into clever virtuosity; unlike Sledge and Norman, O'Brien is fascinated with artifice.

In other instances, however, the metafictional devices open his memoir to dazzling perspectives. In "Speaking of Courage" there is Bowker, home from the war, who circles the town's lake in his Chevy as he remembers with guilt the Vietnam death of Kiowa. Bowker finally "could not talk about it and never would." Following this less than successful story, we read "Notes" and learn that after Vietnam, in 1975, Bowker the person wrote O'Brien. Bowker was unhappy with O'Brien's *If I Die in a Combat Zone*. He proposes that O'Brien write the story we just read. When sent a draft of that story, Bowker responds that too much Vietnam has been left out. O'Brien revises, but before he's finished, Bowker commits suicide. This palimpsest of memoir and story, present and past, profoundly deepens the story to include the writer—and the writing—within the moral consequences of the alienation.

The Vietnam experiences that destroyed Bowker drive O'Brien's writing. This contrast, in turn, illuminates the dilemma faced by many memoirists of war. Can the nightmare

Bowker and O'Brien faced in a Vietnam rice paddy be brought home? If so, how in language can it be owned and publicly acknowledged? Exactly this conflict drives Hemingway's autobiographical story "Soldier's Home." Krebs, returning from World War I in France, wanders aimlessly. Vonnegut, whose echo occasionally is heard in O'Brien's prose, struggles with his fictional account of Billy Pilgrim who struggles, in turn, with how he can tell of his war as a POW in Dresden. Where each author succeeds, his character fails. And, from World War I through Vietnam, authors have resorted to increasing artifice to render the effect of war on character: Hemingway uses Gertrude Stein's stylistic innovations; Vonnegut, the devices of science fiction; O'Brien, the metafictional folding of reality in the fictional. Modern war, which threatens conventional views and the integrity of character, is rendered in difficult formal innovations that bring home to the reader the heretofore unspeakable. O'Brien states the issue for the combat veteran: "memories [of war] might" end in "paralysis or worse" were it not for the "act of writing." And the memoirist's hope: "stories can save us."

But O'Brien also races his own cleverness. Some of the stories (sections of this highly wrought little novel) have depth, emotional power, a dazzling reach. I think especially of the title story and "How to Tell a True War Story," the latter as intelligent as it is profound and one of the most brilliant war memoirs I have read. Other sections, "The Sweetheart of the Song Tra Bong" for example, dissolve into clever artifice. Similarly the center of the book, which is six sections focusing on Kiowa's death, is muddled and inconclusive. The final section, "Field Trip," in which O'Brien returns with his daughter to Vietnam and this field, is so undercut by O'Brien's dissembling about what is and is not true that we cannot trust the climactic act of burying Kiowa's war hatchet. For all its brilliance and emotional grounding, this hybrid of memoir and metafiction does not satisfy one's appetite to hear what happened rendered as it was experienced and is remembered.

Sledge, Norman, and Stephens satisfy that appetite and, in doing so, are no less artful than O'Brien. Their voices ring with responses to the events narratively presented. At the end of the great formal advances of modernism, literary prose falls back to the most central of American cultural imperatives—that of rendering what happened, with honesty, with complexity born of experience and not artifice.

PAMELA SMILEY ON THE ROLE OF THE IDEAL (FEMALE) READER

Jimmy Cross (character) visits Tim O'brien (narrator) years after both have returned from Vietnam. They drink gin, swap memories and look at snapshots of that time when they were both "incredibly soft and young" (29). One photo is the volleyball shot of gray-eyed Martha whom Jimmy Cross loves, but who responded to his expressed intention to carry her upstairs and tie her to his bed (where he'd spend the night touching her knee) by crossing her arms protectively across her chest and saying she didn't "understand how men could do those things ... the things men do" (31).

As O'Brien leaves, Jimmy Cross gives him permission to tell his stories only if they make Cross such a hero that Martha will "read [them] and come begging."

> "Make me out to be a good guy, huh? Brave and handsome, all that stuff. Best platoon leader ever." He hesitated for a second. "And do me a favor. Don't mention anything about ____."
>
> "No," I said. "I won't." (31)

Herein lies the central project of O'Brien's *The Things They Carried*: to make the Marthas who stayed home during the sixties and seventies playing volleyball, going to college, reading Virginia Woolf, to make such women understand their brothers, friends and lovers who went to Vietnam. This O'Brien (the author) accomplishes through a series of female characters—Martha, Mary Anne, Lemon's sister, the woman at the reading, and Linda—through whom he de-genders war, constructs an ideal (female) reader, and re-defines American masculinity.

War fiction is usually less concerned with women than with rituals and tests that "make you a man" (87). The plotting of these—in novels, film, and popular culture—follows genre conventions. First is the separation from women and their "civilizing" influence. Second is the performance of masculinity according to traditional standards involving bravery, physical prowess, and virility. And third is the company of men, particularly the wizened sergeant (or some other father figure) who pronounces the young soldier "a man."

For example, Nick Adams from *In Our Times* (one of the Oedipal works against which *The Things They Carried* plays out its Bloomsian anxiety of influence) wants to silence women having babies, be free of the responsibilities Marjorie brings with her, and be left alone to perform stoically in Seney's burned wasteland. Once separated from women, figures like Rambo (another example) can be pulled from the primordial slime ("look at those pecs! How could that be anything BUT a real man?") to reassure movie-goers that despite the moral swamp of Vietnam and its consequent feminization of America, figures of uncompromised masculinity still exist. (See Jefford's "Masculinity as Excess" for an analysis of this dynamic in Vietnam War films.)

Interestingly, *The Things They Carried* departs radically from these conventions. Mary Anne, in Vietnam, not only fails to "civilize;' but is herself seduced by the war. It is not to a company of men that O'Brien's characters perform, but rather to ideal readers in the form of Lemon's sister and the woman at the reading. And instead of an act of uncompromised masculinity signaling the boy is now a man, O'Brien's character appropriates the feminine, becoming an androgynous fusion of preadolescent Timmy and Linda.

Mary Anne

Against the figure of Martha who crosses her arms against understanding "the things men do," stands Mary Anne, "the sweetheart of Song Tra Bong." Are women less warlike than men because they have breasts and give birth? Mary Anne is O'Brien's argument that the kinder, gentler world of the feminine is nothing but an illusion. As Rat Kiley puts it:

> You got these blinders on about women. How gentle and peaceful they are. All that crap about how if we had a pussy for president there would be no more war. Pure garbage. You got to get rid of that sexist attitude. (117)

Women who never go to war are not innocent so much as they are ignorant of their own capacity for violence. Mary Anne is a test case. She comes to Vietnam right out of high school in "white culottes and this sexy pink sweater": a cliché of the American girl and the female equivalent of Jimmy Cross, Curt Lemon, Kiowa, and the narrator. By the time Mary Anne disappears in the shadows of the jungle, her face is "smooth and vacant" and she wears a "necklace of human tongues" (125).

Mary Anne explains her own awakening in terms of appetite and carnal excitement, of being absolutely in the body.

> Sometimes I want to eat this place. Vietnam. I want to swallow the whole country—the dirt, death—I just want to eat it and have it there inside me ... When I'm out there at night, I feel close to my own body. I can feel my blood moving, my skin and my fingernails, everything. It's like I'm full of electricity and I'm glowing in the dark— I'm on fire almost—I'm burning away into nothing—but it doesn't matter because I know exactly who I am. You can't feel like that anywhere else. (121)

Notice, in contrast, how the (male?) narrator of "How to Tell a True War Story" describes his reaction to war. He does not appetitively ingest the world, does not lose his sense of himself as subject, and instead of a heightened sense of embodiment, feels "out-of-his-skin."

After a firefight, there is always an immense pleasure of

aliveness. The trees are alive. The grass, the soil—everything. All around you things are purely living, and you among them. And the aliveness makes you tremble. You feel an intense, out-of-the-skin awareness of your living self—your truest self, the human being you want to be and then become by force of wanting it. (87)

While it is interesting that O'Brien has his female character taking the world inside her and his male character expanding out to become the world, his point seems to be less the gender stereotypes than the (non-gendered) Dionysian energy common to both descriptions. War destroys order, subverts higher processes such as reason and compassion, and returns us to instinct and our bodies. Such an explosive release allows men and women to be what they might have been without cultural restraints. This O'Brien notes:

A true war story is never moral. It does not instruct nor encourage virtue, nor suggest models of proper human behavior, nor restrain men from doing things men have always done. (76)

Mary Anne illustrates not just the release war brings, but also how women (and this is gender-specific) are "freed" when they travel outside of their culture and its definitions of what it means to be a woman. Think of Isak Dinesen and Beryl Markham and Alexandra David-Neel. This is true especially in Asia, where Western women are accorded the status of honorary men. For Mary Anne such freedom allows her to explore appetite and power—a matrix that has proved a rich vein for feminist exploration. (See, for example, Susan Bordo's *Unbearable Weight*.)

Mary Anne confesses to an appetite so large she could "swallow the whole country." Uncontained woman's appetite=chaos: O'Brien defuses such an equation by couching Mary Anne's appetite in terms of heterosexual sex and pregnancy. Even her necklace of human tongues doesn't carry the horror it could; rather, as is consistent with the rest of *The*

Things They Carried, its violence is seen at a slant. Azar straps a grenade to a puppy. Rat shoots a baby water buffalo. Lemon steals nightgowns from Mama-sans. The only contact with the enemy ends in "the man I killed," a source of grief for the narrator, not a passage into manhood.

Underlying each of the acts listed above, however, is a more serious violence, the unspeakable "____" Jimmy Cross makes the narrator promise not to include. Killing, destruction, rape: the very stuff of the war genre is missing in O'Brien. Mary Anne demonstrates that woman, by virtue of her female body, is not immune to "that mix of unnamed terror and unnamed pleasure that comes as the needle slips in and you know you're risking something" (125), a demonstration that might collapse should Jimmy Cross' "____" be too explicitly filled. In fact, Mary Anne is less persuasive as an argument that "women do these things, too" than she is as an example of "those of us who have done these things are still human. given the situation you'd have done the same." This argument "human, just like you" shifts the normative masculine away from a lethal Dionysian erotic energy to the benign wantonness Azar claims in self-defense: "Christ, I'm just a boy" (40). In post-Vietnam America, masculinity released from the constraints of feminine civilization moves not to Rambo or John Wayne but to Mary Anne and Timmy.

Lemon's Sisters and The Old Woman at the Reading

One such "____" O'Brien elides to avoid the usual stuff of war is Curt Lemon's trick-or-treating. The several tellings of the story and the reaction of Lemon's sister to one version allow O'Brien to construct his ideal reader (a female) through the negative example of the "dumb cooze who never writes back" (76).

Rat Kiley writes a letter to Curt Lemon's sister to tell her "what a great brother she had, how together the guy was, a number one pal and comrade. A real soldier's soldier" (75). Kiley's impulse is the same as Jimmy Cross' "read them and come begging": to use storytelling to win a female reader.

Except that Kiley has not learned the value of "____." He

tells this version of Lemon's trick-or-treating in a letter to the dead man's sister:

> On Halloween, this really hot spooky night, the dude paints his body all different colors and puts on this weird mask and hikes over to the ville and goes trick or treating almost stark naked, just boots and balls and an M-16. (76)

A man lurking in the shadows, the conflation of sexuality and violence ("balls and M-16"), nakedness: these are the details of a rape. Susan Griffin (for one) argues that the real difference between men and women's embodiment is women's constant vigilance against rape, a condition to which Kiley's details betray no sensitivity.

O'Brien, the narrator who is "too smart, too compassionate, too everything... A liberal, for Christ's sake" (45) intervenes and explains Kiley:

> He is nineteen years old and it is too much for him—so he looks at you with those big sad gentle killer eyes and says cooze because his friend is dead, and because it's so incredibly sad and true: she never wrote back. (76–7)

Kiley is the victim: victim of his youth, the press of history, his killer eyes, and of the woman who never wrote back.

Fictionalized acts of reading often signal what an author requires of his/her ideal reader. Here, the "dumb cooze" is a negative example: the ideal woman reader will not be squeamish about sexual violence and will remain open to confessional male voices, particularly those with "sad gentle killer eyes." To judge Lemon is to take Martha's position: crossed arms, refusing to "understand ... the things men do." To not judge is to be open, like Mary Anne.

O'Brien does not deny the subtext of sexual violence. In a later re-telling of the trick-or-treat story Kiley makes explicit the previously implicit female victim.

See what happens is, it's like four in the morning and

Lemon sneaks into a hootch with the weird ghost mask on. Everyone's asleep, right? So he wakes up this cute little Mama-san. Tickles her foot. "Hey Mama-san;' he goes, real soft-like. "Hey Mama-san, trick-or-treat!" Should've seen her face. About freaks. I mean there's this buck naked ghost standing there and he's got this M-16 against her ear and he whispers "Hey Mama-san, trick-or-fucking-treat!" Then he takes off her p.j.s. Strips her right down. Sticks the pajamas in his sack and tucks her into bed and heads for the next hootch. (286)

Rather than deny the violence of Jimmy Cross' "____," O'Brien mitigates it by including other—equally masculine, but often overlooked—"things men do." Jimmy Cross holding a pebble under his tongue. The sunlight lifting Lemon into the canopy of trees. The buzz of the mountains coining alive at sunset. These are the details of a seduction. The seduction of the female reader who must be aware of, at the same time she suspends judgment on, the "____."

"Don't ever mention ____:"

"No" I said. "I won't." (31)

"How to Tell a True War Story" has another female character, "always a woman. Usually it's an older woman of kindly temperament and humane politics" (90). This character, too, is caught by a story, O'Brien's reading of Rat Kiley's killing of the baby water buffalo.

[Rat Kiley] stepped back and shot it through the front knee. The animal did not make a sound. It went down hard, then got up again, and Rat took careful aim and shot off an ear. He shot it twice in the hindquarters and in the little hump at its back ... It wasn't to kill; it was to hurt ... Curt Lemon was dead. Rat Kiley had lost his best friend in the world ... But for now it was a question of pain. (65)

Fury and the blind impulse to cause pain are part of the experience of war. For O'Brien to not include them would strain credibility, but it is his method of detailing these things that distinguishes him. The baby buffalo moment is similar to one of the most disturbing scenes in the movie *Platoon*, in which American soldiers destroy a Vietnamese village after finding their friend crucified on the trail. In O'Brien, the fury is directed at the baby buffalo rather than a village of people, displacing some of the horror while not denying it. And yet the narrator is still acutely sensitive to the reader holding herself apart and judging. The older woman who hears the story explains

> That as a rule she hates war stories; cannot understand why people want to wallow in all the blood and gore. But this one she liked. The poor baby water buffalo, it made her sad. (90)

And the narrator counters that she has not listened. Her sensibility is misplaced. She doesn't get it because the story is "about sunlight ... It's about love and memory" (91).

She has reduced this complex paradox to a cliché of pop self-help psychology. He must, she advises, simply leave it behind and get on with life.

The older woman, like the dumb cooze, is a fictionalized act of reading whereby O'Brien fashions his ideal reader. Jimmy Cross wants Martha to hear his stories and accept them. Rat Kiley wants Lemon's sister to read and understand. O'Brien wants the older woman to hear his love story. Mitchell Sanders generalizes beyond the female reader, but even he eventually circles back and identifies her as his central audience. She is the one who counts.

> Nobody listens. Nobody hears nothin'. Like that fatass colonel. The politicians, all the civilian types. Your girlfriend. My girlfriend. Everybody's sweet little virgin girlfriend. (83)

When a woman listens and understands, something shifts. As a result, the man's experience has—what is it? Reality? Validity? Redemption? Instead of the sergeant who proclaims the soldier a man, it is the ideal female reader for whom O'Brien's characters perform their masculinity.

Linda

Zen-like paradoxes shape this work. "War stories are love stories." "Truth is a lie." A woman is a "virgin and not a virgin." It is no surprise then that O'Brien resolves the collection's project making the Marthas of the world understand; constructing the ideal female reader; giving the male protagonist's experience validity, reality and redemption— through paradox as well. In the final story, "Lives of the Dead" (the title itself a paradox), the narrator pushes each of his previous points to that space outside of the logic we collectively hold to be true. Not only are women (Mary Anne) capable of doing what men do, but also despite men doing the things they do, they remain innocents. Not only does O'Brien construct an ideal female reader, he becomes her in Linda. And redemption lies not in the sergeant's or reader's or lover's witness, but in the very act of creation, the "loops and spins and ... high leaps" of storytelling (273).

O'Brien's narrative success at repressing the usual elements of war—killing, rape, destruction—prepares the way for him to claim that despite the fact that he has killed a man and lived through Vietnam's "Garden of Evil. Over here, man, every sin's real fresh and original" (86), he remains Timmy, his innocent childhood self. The man finds himself in the boy he was, and that self hasn't "changed at all. I was Timmy then; now I'm Tim" (265).

At the end of the Twentieth Century, the meaning of manhood in America is anything but straightforward. Susan Faludi's *Stiffed* is only the most recent in an ongoing conversation that includes *Harper's* cover article, "Are Men Necessary?", the Promise Keepers, Robert Bly, and the Million Man March. This crisis began, some claim, with the Vietnam War generation. Traditional rituals of passage possible for soldiers in World Wars I and II were no longer available to their sons and grandsons. The average age of the "boys" in Vietnam was eighteen.

Manhood, for O'Brien's narrator, is a return to the boy he was. And that boy contains Linda. the girl he loved when he was nine. Now, at forty-three, he speaks to her in dreams, tells her story, imagines her alive.

> And then it becomes 1990. I'm forty-three years old, and a writer now, still dreaming Linda alive in exactly the same way. She's not embodied Linda; she's mostly made up, with a new identity and a new name, like the man who never was ... [I]n the spell of memory and imagination, I can still see her as if through ice, as if I'm gazing into some other world, a place where there are no bodies at all. I can see Kiowa, too, and Ted Lavender and Curt Lemon and sometimes I can even see Timmy skating with Linda under the yellow floodlights. (273)

Unlike Martha who crosses her arms or the dumb cooze who never wrote back, Linda cannot hold herself apart because she is frozen, static, she is Timmy. Her allure is her link to all that is best in Tim. Her threat is the stink of death she carries, the inevitable end of every body. It is usually, Julia Kristeva's "Stabat Mater" argues, women's position to stand between man and death. While this role has a place in *The Things They Carried* (Dobbins with his girlfriend's pantyhose around his neck even after the woman drops him: "no sweat ... The magic doesn't go away" [130]), it is not where O'Brien ends up.

The skating rink's invitation to self-knowledge gestures toward Walden Pond, the tarn near the House of Usher, Ahab's ocean, and the swamp of the Big Two-hearted River. But it's frozen water: a mirror as well as a transparent barrier that both links and separates O'Brien from the dead on whose lives he writes in order to protect Timmy.

> I'm young and I'll never die. I'm skimming across the surface of my own history, moving fast, riding the melt

beneath the blades, doing loops and spins, and when I take high leaps into the dark and come down thirty years later, I realize it's Tim trying to save Timmy's life with a story. (273)

"I'll never die." These are the very words the young boy in Hemingway's "Indian Camp" believes when he returns with his father (a doctor) from a particularly difficult birthing.

They were seated in the boat, Nick in the stern, his father rowing. The sun was coming over the hills. A bass jumped, making a circle in the water. Nick trailed his hand in the water. It felt warm in the sharp chill of the morning. In the early morning on the lake sitting in the stern of the boat with his father rowing, he felt quite sure that he would never die. ("Indian Camp" 19)

Both Hemingway and O'Brien evoke the moment at which the boy enters the secret circle of manhood. The difference is that Hemingway's character leaves the woman behind in the Indian camp, O'Brien's freezes her and makes the ice the surface on which the protective circle of manhood is composed.

In the final paragraph of O'Brien's collection, Linda lies frozen beneath the ice on which O'Brien "loops and spins" his stories. "Not dead," Linda explains in a dream. "But when I am, it's like ... I don't know, I guess it's like being inside a book nobody's reading" (273). Linda's death, O'Brien's absorption of and recreation of her, the self-protective distance denied the "dumb cooze": these "____" aren't a whole lot different from woman as blank sheet, nature fashioned into culture, the raw stuff of men's art—all those boringly familiar and too predictable functions of women's place in men's art. Too obvious to even deserve comment.

More interesting is the question, why do women readers play? Why would any woman reader want to become O'Brien's ideal, given the conditions he sets? The answer, I believe, lies not so much in the genre of war literature as it does in the gothic.

At the climax of the gothic, the hero (heretofore a public figure of great power who has amused himself by torturing and toying with a female innocent, the protagonist) realizes the woman he has been victimizing is not peripheral to his life, but its very center. She is his soul. His meaning. And he surrenders to her. A Heathcliffian love.

As in all effective gothics, the love in *The Things They Carried* is at once both hotly sexual and intensely spiritual. Jimmy Cross wants to

> Sleep inside [Martha's] lungs and breathe her blood. Be smothered. He wanted her to be a virgin and not a virgin all at once. He wanted to know her intimate secrets ... (12)

And nine-year old Timmy "wanted to live inside [Linda's] body. I wanted to melt into her bones—that kind of love" (258).

This fusion of woman and man is not the stuff of Woodstock and the casual sex of the Pill. This is not daily shopping lists and three o'clock feedings and the toilet seat (up? down?). This is a love of epic proportions in which soul mates merge and their union contains everything. In an age that takes sex and love so lightly, this is an exceptional claim to make for the love of a woman. That she is the means of spiritual redemption. That only through her can life become whole. No wonder O'Brien writes, "It wasn't a war story. It was a love story" (90). No wonder women read him. Where else in post-Vietnam American culture is a woman's love worth so much?

Works Cited

Susan Griffin, "Rape and the Power of Consciousness" in *Issues in Feminism*. Ed. Sheila Ruth. London: Mayfield Publishers 1995, 285–295.

Ernest Hemingway, "Indian Camp" from *In Our Time*. New York: Collier Books, 1925.

Susan Jeffords, "Masculinity as Excess in Vietnam Films: The Father–Son Dynamic of American Culture" in *Feminisms: An Anthology of Literary*

Theory and Criticism. Ed. Robyn R. Warhol and Diane Price Herndl. New Brunswick, New Jersey: Rutgers UP, 1991.

Julia Kristeva, "Stabat Mater," in *Tales of Love*. Trans. Leon S. Roudiez. New York: Columbia University Press, 1987.

Tim O'Brien, *The Things They Carried: A Work of Fiction*. Boston: Houghton Mifflin, 1990.

ROBIN BLYN ON O'BRIEN'S
THE THINGS THEY CARRIED

"But this too is true," Tim O'Brien's narrator insists in the first line of the chapter that concludes *The Things They Carried*: "Stories can save us" (224). Entitled "The Lives of the Dead," this final chapter thus begins with a promise not only of healing, but of redemption as well. Stories, the narrator suggests, can heal the traumatized veteran of the Vietnam War and provoke an amnesiac nation into "working through" its troubled past. If, as John Hellemann has written, "the legacy of Vietnam is the disruption of our story, of our explanation of the past and vision of the future" (x), then O'Brien's narrator apparently points "the disrupted story" and the nation toward a narrative cure. Such a reading of *The Things They Carried*, however, requires a denial of the novel's insistent destabilization of the "true" and its dogged attempts to render war unequivocally beyond redemption. Shifting attention from the final chapter's first line to its concluding passage makes visible the extent to which the novel challenges the narrative cure that its narrator ostensibly affirms.

The idea of stories as a curative force is attractive, particularly because it suggests that, as a collection of stories about American soldiers in Vietnam, *The Things They Carried* performs the narrative cure it prescribes, redeeming the reader and the writer at once. Prepared to be "saved," the producer and the receiver of the stories are poised for the closure traditionally accomplished in the final chapter of a war story. For, as Paul Fussell explains in his *The Great War and Modern Memory*, the third and final stage of the war narrative is the "reconsideration," in which the prewar understanding of the world is replaced by the deeper insights made painfully clear by the war experience (130). Closure entails both a loss of innocence and redemption in the form of a richer appreciation for the complexities of the human condition. By beginning the final chapter with an assertion that "stories can save us," O'Brien apparently promises just this kind of "reconsideration." To the contrary, however, the chapter concludes with an image of suspension and spin that reflects a profound sense of cultural ambiguity. It is an image that recalls the critique of narrative structure first undertaken in chapter 3, aptly entitled "Spin," and expanded on four chapters later in "How to Tell a True War Story."

At the end of "The Lives of the Dead," an older "Tim" imagines a younger "Timmy" skating on a frozen lake with his childhood sweetheart, Linda. Tim writes:

> I'm young and happy. I'll never die. I'm skimming across the surface of my own history, moving fast, riding the melt beneath the blades, doing loops and spins, and when I take a high leap into the dark and come down thirty years later, I realize it is as Tim trying to save Timmy's life with a story. (246)

Because this is the passage with which the novel concludes, the question of whether or not Tim is ultimately able to save his younger self "with a story" remains unresolved. Moreover, the reference to "loops" and "spins" links this image both to the circular path of memory and to the problem of the narrative "spin" known as "the war story." In the chapter entitled "Spin," the unending repetitions of the memory "loop" function as a check against the falsifications of the war story and its conventional "spins."

As a chapter, "Spin" exposes the desire that generates the genre of the war story, a dangerous and insipid desire to redeem what the narrator calls the "waste" of war (68). Like "The Lives of the Dead," it begins with a statement that the rest of the chapter throws into question. "The War wasn't all terror and violence," the narrator tells us, "Sometimes things could almost get sweet" (31). What follows, however, is a series of vignettes that are anything but "sweet." When a Vietnamese boy with a plastic leg approaches an American soldier with a chocolate bar, the soldier reflects, "One leg, for Chrissake. Some poor fucker ran out of ammo" (31). When the same soldier steals his friend's puppy, "strapped it to a Claymore antipersonnel mine and squeezed the firing device," he responds with an ironic affirmation of the initiation right of the conventional war story: "What's everyone so upset about? ... I mean, Christ, I'm just a boy" (37). Here, the novel renders ironic both the loss of innocence and the "reconsideration" that structure the traditional war story. The positive spin that underlies the war story as a genre emerges here only as a bankrupt fantasy. Thus in "How to Tell a True War Story," the narrator warns, "If a story seems moral, do not believe it. If at the end of a war story you feel uplifted, or if you feel that some small bit of rectitude has been salvaged from the larger waste, then you have been made the victim of a very old and terrible lie" (68). Aimed at exposing this "old and terrible lie," these chapters refute any narrative structure that would redeem the war, the storyteller, or the audience to which it is directed.

Against the comforts and closure of the war story, "Spin" reveals the circular repetitions and reenactments of traumatic memory. In "Spin," memory itself is depicted as a loop:

> The memory-traffic feeds into a rotary up on your head, where it goes in circles for a while, then pretty soon imagination flows in and the traffic merges and shoots down a thousand different streets. As a writer, all you can do is pick a street and go for the ride, putting things down as they come at you. That's the real obsession. All those stories. (35)

Evoking the compulsive repetitions of traumatic memory, the narrator here characterizes stories not as the road to closure, but as "obsession," a kind of psychological "traffic." Effectively, this loop describes the structure of "Spin" and of

The Things They Carried as a whole. For in place of tales of moral uplift and the persistence of human goodness, tales structured to provide the catharsis of Aristotelian tragedy, "Spin" offers the ambiguous, the unfinished, and the wound that will not succumb to the narrative cure. Keeping the wound open, O'Brien's text prevents the neat closure and false redemption of the traditional war story.

Given that the "spin" and the "loop" are terms central to the novel's critique of war stories and their specious attempts to reclaim meaning from the war experience, the final passage of "The Lives of the Dead" may be seen as a direct challenge to the sentence that begins it. Rather than confirming that "stories can save us" by redeeming the past and healing all wounds, Timmy's acrobatic performance on the frozen pond may be seen as a reiteration of the "memory-traffic" (35) and its obsessive art. Prohibiting closure, *The Things They Carried* keeps the past from disappearing into the dead clichés of the war story, replacing redemption with a critical engagement with the past.

Works Cited

Fussell, Paul. *The Great War and Modern Memory*. New York: Oxford UP, 1975.

Hellemann, John. *American Myth and the Legacy of Vietnam*. New York: Columbia UP, 1986.

O'Brien, Tim. *The Things They Carried*. New York: Broadway, 1990.

CATHERINE CALLOWAY ON 'HOW TO TELL A TRUE WAR STORY': METAFICTION IN *THE THINGS THEY CARRIED*

What exactly is *The Things They Carried* in terms of technique? Many reviewers refer to the work as a series of short stories, but it is much more than that. *The Things They Carried* is a combat novel, yet it is not a combat novel. It is also a blend of traditional and untraditional forms—a collection, Gene Lyons says, of "short stories, essays, anecdotes, narrative fragments, jokes, fables, biographical and autobiographical sketches, and philosophical asides" (52). It has been called both "a unified narrative with chapters that stand perfectly on their own" (Coffey 60) and a series of "22 discontinuous sections" (Bawer A13).

Also ambiguous is the issue of how much of the book is autobiography. The relationship between fiction and reality arises early in the text when the reader learns the first of many parallels that emerge as the book progresses: that the protagonist and narrator, like the real author of *The Things They Carried*, is named Tim O'Brien. Both the real and the fictional Tim O'Brien are in their forties and are natives of Minnesota, writers who graduated Phi Beta Kappa from Macalester College, served as grunts in Vietnam after having been drafted at age twenty-one, attended graduate school at Harvard University, and wrote books entitled *If I Die in a Combat Zone* and *Going After Cacciato*. Other events of the protagonist's life are apparently invention. Unlike the real Tim O'Brien, the protagonist has a nine-year-old daughter named Kathleen and makes a return journey to Vietnam years after the war is over.[1] However, even the other supposedly fictional characters of the book sound real because of an epigraph preceding the stories that states, "This book is lovingly dedicated to the men of Alpha Company, and in particular to Jimmy Cross, Norman Bowker, Rat Kiley, Mitchell Sanders, Henry Dobbins, and Kiowa," leading the reader to wonder if the men of Alpha Company are real or imaginary.

Clearly O'Brien resists a simplistic classification of his latest work. In both the preface to the book and in an interview with Elizabeth Mehren, he terms *The Things They Carried* "'fiction ... a novel'" (Mehren E1), but in an interview with Martin Naparsteck, he refers to the work as a "sort of half novel, half group of stories. It's part nonfiction, too," he insists (7). And, as Naparsteck points out, the work "resists easy categorization: it is part novel, part collection of stories, part essays, part journalism; it is, more significantly, all at the same time" (1).

As O'Brien's extensive focus on storytelling indicates, *The Things They Carried* is also a work of contemporary metafiction, what Robert Scholes first termed fabulation or "ethically controlled fantasy" (3). According to Patricia Waugh,

> *Metafiction* is a term given to fictional writing which self-consciously and systematically draws attention to its status as an artefact in order to pose questions about the relationship between fiction and reality. In providing a critique of their own methods of construction, such writings not only examine the fundamental structures of narrative fiction, they also explore the possible fictionality of the world outside the literary fictional text. (2)

Like O'Brien's earlier novel, the critically acclaimed *Going After Cacciato*,[2] *The Things They Carried* considers the process of writing; it is, in fact, as much about the process of writing as it is the text of a literary work. By examining imagination and memory, two main components that O'Brien feels are important to a writer of fiction (Schroeder 143), and by providing so many layers of technique in one work, O'Brien delves into the origins of fictional creation. In focusing so extensively on what a war story is or is not, O'Brien writes a war story as he examines the process of writing one. To echo what Philip Beidler has stated about *Going After Cacciato*, "the form" of *The Things They Carried* thus becomes "its content" (172); the medium becomes the message.

"I'm forty-three years old, and a writer now," O'Brien's protagonist states periodically throughout the book, directly referring to his role as author and to the status of his work as artifice. "Much of it [the war] is hard to remember," he comments. "I sit at this typewriter and stare through my words and watch Kiowa sinking into the deep muck of a shit field, or Curt Lemon hanging in pieces from a tree, and as I write about these things, the remembering is turned into a kind of rehappening" (36). The "rehappening" takes the form of a number of types of stories: some happy, some sad, some peaceful, some bloody, some wacky. We learn of Ted Lavender, who is "zapped while zipping" (17) after urinating, of the paranoid friendship of Dave Jensen and Lee Strunk, of the revenge plot against Bobby Jorgenson, an unskilled medic who almost accidentally kills the narrator, of the moral confusion of the protagonist who fishes on the Rainy River and dreams of desertion to Canada, and Mary Anne Bell, Mark Fossie's blue-eyed, blonde, seventeen-year-old girlfriend, who is chillingly attracted to life in a combat zone.

Some stories only indirectly reflect the process of writing; other selections include obvious metafictional devices. In certain sections of the book, entire chapters are devoted to discussing form and technique. A good example is "Notes," which elaborates on "Speaking of Courage," the story that precedes it. The serious reader of the real Tim O'Brien's fiction recognizes "Speaking of Courage" as having first been published in the Summer 1976 issue of *Massachusetts Review*.[3] This earlier version of the story plays off chapter 14 of *Going After Cacciato*, "Upon Almost Winning the Silver Star," in which the protagonist, Paul Berlin, is thinking about how he might have won the Silver Star for bravery in Vietnam had he had the courage to rescue Frenchie Tucker, a character shot while searching a tunnel. However, in *The Things They Carried*'s version of "Speaking of Courage," the protagonist is not Paul Berlin, but Norman Bowker, who wishes he had had the courage to save Kiowa, a soldier who dies in a field of excrement during a mortar attack.[4] Such shifts in character and events tempt the reader into textual participation, leading him to question the ambiguous nature of reality. Who really did not win the Silver Star for bravery? Paul Berlin, Norman Bowker, or Tim O'Brien? Who actually needed saving? Frenchie Tucker or Kiowa? Which version of the story, if either, is accurate? The inclusion of a metafictional chapter presenting the background behind the tale provides no definite answers or resolutions. We learn that Norman Bowker, who eventually commits suicide, asks the narrator to compose the story and that the author has revised the tale for inclusion in *The Things They Carried* because a postwar story is more appropriate for the later book than for *Going After Cacciato*. However, O'Brien's admission that much of the story is still invention compels the reader to wonder about the truth. The narrator assures us that the truth is that "Norman did not experience a failure of nerve that night ... or lose the Silver Star for valor" (182). Can even this version be believed? Was there really a Norman Bowker, or is he, too, only fictional?

Even more significant, the reader is led to question the reality of many, if not all, of the stories in the book. The narrator insists that the story of Curt Lemon's death, for instance, is "all exactly true" (77), then states eight pages later that he has told Curt's story previously—"many times, many versions" (85)—before narrating yet another version. As a result, any and all accounts of the incident are questionable. Similarly, the reader is led to doubt the validity of many of the tales told by other characters in the book. The narrator remarks that Rat Kiley's stories, such as the one about Mary Anne Bell in "Sweetheart of the Song Tra Bong," are particularly ambiguous:

> For Rat Kiley ... facts were formed by sensation, not the other way around, and when you listened to one of his stories, you'd find yourself performing rapid calculations in your head, subtracting superlatives, figuring the square root of an absolute and then multiplying by maybe. (101)

Still other characters admit the fictionality of their stories. Mitchell Sanders, in the ironically titled "How to Tell a True War Story," confesses to the protagonist that although his tale is the truth, parts of it are pure invention. "'Last night, man,'" Sanders states, "'I had to make up a few things ... The glee club. There wasn't any glee club ... No opera,'" either (83–84). "'But,'" he adds, "'it's still true'" (84).

O'Brien shares the criteria with which the writer or teller and the reader or listener must be concerned by giving an extended definition of what a war story is or is not. The chapter "How to Tell a True War Story" focuses most extensively on the features that might be found in a "true" war tale. "A true war story is never moral," the narrator states. "It does not instruct, nor encourage virtue, nor suggest models of proper human behavior, nor restrain men from doing the things men have always done" (76). Furthermore, a true war story has an "absolute and uncompromising allegiance to obscenity and evil" (76), is embarrassing, may not be believable, seems to go on forever, does "not generalize" or "indulge in abstraction or analysis" (84), does not necessarily make "a point" (88), and sometimes cannot even be told. True war stories, the reader soon realizes, are like the nature of the Vietnam War itself; "the only certainty is overwhelming ambiguity" (88). "The final and definitive truth" (83) cannot be derived, and any "truths are contradictory" (87).

By defining a war story so broadly, O'Brien writes more stories, interspersing the definitions with examples from the war to illustrate them. What is particularly significant about the examples is that they are given in segments, a technique that actively engages the readers in the process of textual creation. Characters who are mentioned as having died early in the work are brought back to life through flashbacks in other parts of the text so that we can see who these characters are, what they are like, and how they die. For instance, in the story, "Spin," the narrator first refers to the death of Curt Lemon, a soldier blown apart by a booby trap, but the reader does not learn the details of the tragedy until four stories later in "How to Tell a True War Story." Even then, the reader must piece together the details of Curt's death throughout that particular tale. The first reference to Lemon appears on the third page of the story when O'Brien matter-of-factly states, "The dead guy's name was Curt Lemon" (77). Lemon's death is briefly mentioned a few paragraphs later, but additional details surrounding the incident are not given at once but are revealed gradually throughout the story, in between digressive stories narrated by two other soldiers, Rat Kiley and Mitchell Sanders. Each fragment about Curt's accident illustrates the situation more graphically. Near the beginning of the tale, O'Brien describes the death somewhat poetically. Curt is "a handsome kid, really. Sharp grey eyes, lean and narrow-waisted, and when he died it was almost beautiful, the way the sunlight came around him and lifted him up and sucked him high into a tree full of moss and vines and white blossoms" (78). Lemon is not mentioned again for seven pages, at which time O'Brien illustrates the effect of Lemon's death upon the other soldiers by detailing how Rat Kiley, avenging Curt's death, mutilates and kills a baby water buffalo. When later in the story Lemon's accident is narrated for the third time, the reader is finally told what was briefly alluded to in the earlier tale "Spin": how the soldiers had to peel Curt Lemon's body parts from a tree.

The story of Curt Lemon does not end with "How to Tell a True War Story" but is narrated further in two other stories, "The Dentist" and "The Lives of the Dead." In "The Lives of the Dead," for example, Curt is resurrected through a story of his trick-or-treating in Vietnamese hootches on Halloween for whatever goodies he can get: "candles and joss sticks and a pair of black pajamas and statuettes of the smiling Buddha" (268). To hear Rat Kiley tell it, the narrator comments, "you'd never know that Curt Lemon was dead. He was still out there in the dark, naked and painted up, trick-or-treating, sliding from hootch to hootch in that crazy white ghost mask" (268). To further complicate matters, in "The Lives of the Dead," O'Brien alludes to a soldier other than Curt, Stink Harris, from a previous literary work, *Going After Cacciato*, written over a decade before *The Things They Carried*. Thus, the epistemological uncertainty in the stories is mirrored by the fact that O'Brien presents events that take place in a fragmented form rather than in a straightforward, linear fashion. The reader has to piece together information, such as the circumstances surrounding the characters' deaths, in the same manner that the characters must piece together the reality of the war, or, for that matter, Curt Lemon's body.

Notes

1. Biographical information on the real Tim O'Brien is taken from published facts of his life. See, for instance, Michael Coffey, "Tim O'Brien", *Publishers Weekly*, 237, 16 Feb. 1990, 60–61, and Everett C. Wilkie, Jr., "Tim O'Brien," *Dictionary of Literary Biography Yearbook: 1980*,

eds. Karen L. Rood, Jean W. Ross, and Richard Ziegfeld. Detroit: Gale, 1981, 286–290.

2. New York: Delta/Seymour Lawrence, 1978. *Going After Cacciato* received the National Book Award in 1979.

3. Vol. 17, pp. 243–253. The earlier version of the story has also been published in *Prize Stories 1978: The O'Henry Awards*. Ed. and intro. William Abrahams. Garden City: Doubleday, 1978, 159–168. A later version of "Speaking of Courage" appeared in *Granta*, 29 (Winter 1989): 135–154. along with "Notes."

4. O'Brien frequently makes changes between versions of his stories that are published in literary magazines and chapters of his books. The version of "Spin" that was published in the Spring 1990 issue of *The Quarterly* (3–13), for example, combines several of the individual stories from *The Things They Carried* into one longer tale. In addition, O'Brien makes changes between the hardback and paperback versions of his books. In both the "Field Trip" chapter of the hardback edition of *The Things They Carried* and the short story version of "Field Trip" (*McCalls* 17, August 1990: 78–79), the narrator returns Kiowa's hatchet to the site of Kiowa's death, but in the paperback edition of *The Things They Carried* (New York: Penguin, 1990), the narrator carries a pair of Kiowa's moccasins. For references to changes in O'Brien's earlier works, see my "Pluralities of Vision: *Going After Cacciato* and Tim O'Brien's Short Fiction," *America Rediscovered: Critical Essays on Literature and Film of the Vietnam War*. Eds. Owen W. Gilman, Jr. and Lorrie Smith. New York: Garland, 1990, 213–224.

MARIA S. BONN ON TIM O'BRIEN AND THE EFFICACY OF THE TEXT

In this novel, the relationship between truth and fiction and the consideration of the effective potential of stories has moved to center stage. In person and in interviews O'Brien presents himself as a bluff ordinary guy, who claims his literary influences are "'the books I read as a kid. *The Hardy Boys* and Larry of the Little League'" (Lyons 52) and who has little interest in aesthetic theory. But his work belies this stance. When asked if *The Things They Carried* is nonfiction O'Brien appears startled by the question and says off-handedly that every bit of it is fiction. Yet the narrator of *The Things They*

Carried is a forty-three-year-old Vietnam veteran named Tim O'Brien who has previously written a memoir called *If I Die in a Combat Zone* and the novel entitled *Going After Cacciato.*

An examination of even the prefatory material to *The Things They Carried* reveals that O'Brien is far more of a literary trickster than he acknowledges. The title page asserts the novel is "a work of fiction by Tim O'Brien." It is followed by a disclaimer that "this is a work of fiction. Except for a few details regarding the author's own life, all the incidents, names, and characters are imaginary." So far this is clear enough. But by the dedication page O'Brien is already beginning to muddy the textual waters. The book is dedicated to "the men of Alpha Company"; the dedication goes on to list their names. They are the names of the characters of *The Things They Carried.*

In and of itself this dedication to fictional characters might be passed over as whimsy on O'Brien's part, but it is soon revealed as part of the novel's elaborate interlocking pattern of truth and fiction. For example, in "Notes" O'Brien tells us that the story "Speaking of Courage" was written at the suggestion of Norman Bowker, one of those fictional men of Alpha Company, who wrote to O'Brien after reading *If I Die in a Combat Zone.* "The Sweetheart of the Song Tra Bong," one of the most apparently fictive of the twenty-one pieces that make up *The Things They Carried,* is based, according to O'Brien, on a story told to him by a battlefield medic in Vietnam, who was "'desperate to make me believe him'" (Lyons 52). The instructive piece "How to Tell a True War Story"—which begins by helpfully reporting "this is true" (75)—explicates: "a true war story cannot be believed. If you believe it, be skeptical" (79). Clearly O'Brien is nudging his readers to question some of their assumptions about fiction and truth.

The three consecutive pieces "Speaking of Courage," "Notes," and "In the Field," exemplify O'Brien's relentless investigation of how to tell a true war story. The first story relates how the character Norman Bowker is unable to save Kiowa, a comrade who suffocates in the muck of excrement when Alpha Company is pinned down in a field full of night soil. In "Notes" the author-character Tim O'Brien tells us that the story was originally written at the suggestion of Norman Bowker who was dissatisfied with *If I Die In a Combat Zone*. As originally published the story featured Paul Berlin of *Going After Cacciato* and was only about the after-effects of the night in the night-soil field and did not discuss the incident itself. The intertextuality thickens. The fictional Norman Bowker expresses further dissatisfaction; he later kills himself. Prompted by the suicide, the author-character O'Brien rewrites the story for inclusion in *The Things They Carried*. The record is set straight—until the conclusion of "Notes" where O'Brien reports: "in the interests of truth, however, I want to make it clear that Norman Bowker was in no way responsible for what happened to Kiowa ... that part of the story is my own" (182). "In the Field" then is the final elucidation, the story in which O'Brien explains that he, not Norman Bowker, was the friend unable to save Kiowa that night.

Lest his readers should be tempted to believe that with "In the Field" they have at last been granted a definitive or foundational story, O'Brien follows that story with "Good Form," another authorial commentary by the character Tim O'Brien. It opens with the statement "it's time to be blunt"— surely an alarming declaration to readers that have been struggling through the book's labyrinth of truth. He then goes on:

> I'm forty-three years old, true, and I'm a writer now, and a long time ago I walked through the Quang Ngai Province as a foot soldier.
>
> Almost everything else is invented.
>
> But it's not a game. It's a form. Right here, right now, as I invent myself, I'm thinking of all I want to tell you about why this book is written as it is. For instance, I want to tell you this: twenty years ago I watched a man die on a trail near the village of My Khe. I did not kill him. But I was present you see, and my presence was guilt enough I blamed myself. And rightly so, because I was present.
>
> But listen. Even that story is made up. (203)

So much for being blunt. But the dizzying interplay of truth and fiction in this novel is not solely aesthetic postmodern gamesmanship but a form that is a thematic continuation of the author's concern throughout his career with the power and capability of story.

The Things They Carried is more polished and manipulative even than the sophisticated triple play of *Going After Cacciato*. But for all its interrogation of the liminal space between lived experience and imagination and for all its insistence on abjuring any notion of static truth it is still finally more definitive about the potential of the story than either of O'Brien's earlier Vietnam War works. At the end of *Going After Cacciato* Paul Berlin has found a way of making use of war stories to define his moral position, but *The Things They Carried* makes a renewed attack on war stories: "A true war story is never moral. It does not instruct, nor encourage virtue, nor suggest models of proper behavior ... as a first rule of thumb, therefore, you can tell a true war story by its absolute and uncompromising allegiance to obscenity and evil" (76).

Yet at the same time that O'Brien strongly rejects any didactic moral function; for war stories he clarifies his position on just what stories *can* do. Early on he declares that "sometimes remembering will lead to a story, which makes it forever. That's what stories are for. Stories are for joining the past to the future" (40), and he later muses "what stories can do, I guess, is make things present" (204). Story's ability to "make things present" is O'Brien's apparent resolution of the ambivalence toward fiction that has driven him through his Vietnam War books. He has been troubled by the question of whether dreams offer lessons. In *The Things They Carried* he sees his dreams and stories not as lessons but as elegies; they do not teach, but they do preserve.

In Vietnam, O'Brien tells us, "we kept the dead alive with stories" (267). "The Lives of the Dead," the novel's final story contains O'Brien's most definitive articulation of the relationship between memory and story. O'Brien recalls the death of his childhood sweetheart and how night after night he would invent dreams to bring her back. He recalls a conversation in one such dream:

> "Right now," she said, "I'm not dead. But when I am, it's like ... I don't know, I guess it's like being inside a book that nobody's reading."
> "A book?" I said.
> "An old one. It's up on the library shelf, so you're safe and everything, but the book hasn't been checked out for a long, long time. All you can do is wait. Just hope somebody'll pick it up and start reading." (273)

So stories can save us, but through preservation rather than through salvation. In *If I Die in a Combat Zone* O'Brien rejected "the lessons of dead men," and in *The Things They Carried* reading becomes a way of dreaming those dead men back to life. The flesh is made back into word.

O'Brien's Vietnam War works persistently deconstruct the distinctions between memory and imagination, lessons and dreams, truth and fiction, and reality and the text. But the final movement in *The Things They Carried* is toward reconstruction—not of distinctions but rather of a creative connection that draws together experience and art. For O'Brien, stories are that privileged connection that can lift us out of the quagmire of a dualized reality and fantasy and place us on the solid ground of truth. But even this apparent resolution is finally suspended. Because the novel offers us a double lesson: Stories can save us. But if O'Brien's readers have truly accepted his wily postmodern perceptions of the reader's relationship to the text then they know that they must reject any lessons. O'Brien warns "if at the end of a war story you feel uplifted, or if you feel that some small bit of rectitude has been salvaged from the larger waste, then you have been the victim of a very old and terrible lie" (76). So any sense of conclusion or epiphany must be its own undoing. And as O'Brien might say, "this is true."

LORRIE N. SMITH ON THE GENDERED SUBTEXT IN TIM O'BRIEN'S *ESQUIRE* STORIES

V

Rat Kiley figures prominently again as the authoritative witness of the book's most disturbing story, "Sweetheart of the Song Tra Bong." Premised on an elaborately far-fetched "what if," the story unsettles and stretches our ability to suspend disbelief precisely *because* it is calculated to overturn conventional gender roles: suppose a soldier were to "ship his honey over to Nam ... import [his] own personal poontang." The absolute incongruity of having a woman enter the male sanctuary of war reinforces the extent to which culture constructs war as an all-male activity. The story counts on the reader's cognitive dissonance when faced with this image and trades heavily on its novelty and shock effect. As usual, O'Brien layers and fractures his narrative and mixes tones—strategies that mask the gender drama with a struggle over epistemological uncertainty and aesthetic indeterminacy. Framed by the narrator but close to Rat's perspective, the story follows Rat's effort to get it right, to "bracket the full range of meaning" for his incredulous friends. But Rat's story, part of which he heard second-hand and part of which he experienced, comes with the narrator's disclaimer that Rat has a reputation for "exaggeration and overstatement" and may be biased because he "loved her." By the end, the story has the feel of a truth-is-stranger-than-fiction tale in the oral culture of soldiers—the kind of story usually punctuated at the end with the enigmatic "there it is." Within the self-reflexive frame of the story, the actions Rat recounts for the narrator may or may not have happened; as always in this book, we are cautioned against looking for mimetic or factual truth and led toward accepting the emotional truth constructed by the imagination. To the interlocutors within the text, and to the narrator who is almost always complicit with his own characters, this has the ring of a "true war story" because it solidifies the masculine hegemony of war and casts out the monstrous woman who dares to appropriate masculine codes of behavior.

"Sweetheart of the Song Tra Bong" is further complicated by its literary self-consciousness, for it can be read as a gendered and perhaps parodic version of *Heart of Darkness* and its derivative retelling, *Apocalypse Now*—those explorations of the imperialist male psyche gone off the deep end. Here, inscrutable evil and cultural otherness are collapsed into the figure of a woman. The story is less concerned with what motivates the Kurtz figure, however, than with defending men's homosocial bonds against all threat of feminine invasion. As in other *Esquire* stories, the figure of a woman is the other against which masculine identity and innocence are sympathetically defined. Here, though, the woman is distinctly not, as Rat points out, like "all those girls back home, how clean and innocent they all are, how they'll never understand any of this, not in a billion years" (123). O'Brien's ingenious twist is to create a woman who understands war because "she was there. She was up to her eyeballs in it." Of course, being there and understanding war are only conceived in masculine terms—fighting—rather than any of the other roles women actually did play in Vietnam, for the masculine point of view prevails here. The story appears to be deconstructing gender difference by imagining a woman warrior, suggesting that *even* women can be corrupted by war. In fact, though, it portrays the woman as *more* masculine than the men, hence monstrous and unnatural. She can finally be tamed only within a masculine narrative. Characteristically, Rat gives the story a moral: "You come over clean and you get dirty and then afterward it's never the same. A question of degree" (123). The "degree" to which people are transformed by war, however, turns on the difference of gender in this story. Gender difference temporarily blurs but ultimately gets resolved into the old oppositions, and women are warned against disrupting patriarchal order and assuming power assigned to men.

Rat's story takes place at an obscure outpost where he once served as medic, a liminal place where the men are free to bend military rules, where basketball, beer, and easy camaraderie help pass the time between incoming emergencies. Beyond the medical station is a Green Beret base inhabited by six

"Greenies," who are "not social animals." This positioning is significant, for it begins to define "normal" and transgressive behavior in the story. The Greenies are associated with nature; Rat claims they were "animals ... but far from social." Exuding an almost supernatural aura of power and authority, the special forces disappear and then "magically reappear, moving like shadows through the moonlight, filing in silently from the dense rain forest off to the west." The medics keep their distance and "no one asked questions." The base's NCO, Eddie Diamond, sets the plot in motion with a "joke": "What they should do, Eddie said, was pool some bucks and bring in a few mama-sans from Saigon, spice things up." Mark Fossie, a young medic, is taken with the idea, saying that all it would take is "a pair of solid brass balls." The phallic reference is reiterated when Eddie Diamond "told him he'd best strap down his dick." Six weeks later, the men are astonished when Mark's childhood sweetheart, Mary Anne Bell, shows up. After a heavy silence, someone says, simply, "That fucker."

In the beginning, Mary Anne is represented as a parody of the all-American gift and "sweetheart" pin-up, both innocent and sexual. Seventeen and "just barely out of high school," she shows up in "white culottes and this sexy pink sweater." Rat dwells on the details of her appearance: "long white legs and blue eyes and a complexion like strawberry ice cream." She and Mark dote on each other, sharing their American dream of a perfect house, a perfect family, a perfect future. They set up house "in one of the bunkers along the perimeter," on the border between civilization and the Greenies' wilderness. No mere sex symbol, however, Mary Anne has "a bubbly personality" and "a quick mind," and she quickly develops an interest in the art of jungle warfare. Her interest is seen as naive at first, for she seems comically unaware of danger. Eddie Diamond comments, "D-cup guts, trainer-bra brains" but then warns ominously, "this girl will most definitely learn." Unlike all the other women in the book, Mary Anne asks questions and listens carefully. Her interest, however, has nothing to do with strategy or politics. Clearly, she is stimulated by entry to a place both exotic and masculine, beyond the constrictive boundaries of conventional society: "The war intrigued her. The land, too, and the mystery." In his description, which reveals a protective sort of love for Mary Anne, Rat simultaneously erases and calls attention to gender difference: "Like you and me. A *girl*, that's the only difference, and I'll tell you something: it didn't amount to jack. I mean, when we first got here—all of us—we were real young and innocent, full of romantic bullshit, but we learned pretty damn quick. And so did Mary Anne" (108). Like Conrad's dark continent, "Nam" is represented as an external force that changes innocent Westerners forever.

As Mary Anne "learns" about Vietnam, the narrator's descriptions change from conventionally feminine to more masculine terms: she displays "tight, intelligent focus," "confidence in her voice, a new authority in the way she carried herself." Mark is first proud and amazed at her competence, then uncomfortable and angry. "Her body seemed foreign somehow—too stiff in places, too firm where the softness used to be. The bubbliness was gone. The nervous giggling, too" (110). As in other stories, the male's confusion is explained by the fact that he's "just a boy—eighteen years old" (111). Mary Anne starts helping out in the operating room, learning how to fire an M-16, and eventually disappearing at night. At first Mark thinks she's sleeping with someone else, but eventually discovers the incredible fact that "Mary Anne's out on fuckin' *ambush*" with the Greenies. When she first returns from such a mission, Mark "had trouble recognizing her. She wore a bush hat and filthy green fatigues; she carried the standard M-16 automatic assault rifle; her face was black with charcoal" (113), and from this point on the narrative emphasizes how much she changes and how disruptive these changes are to masculine identity and community. Mark temporarily re-establishes patriarchal order by announcing their engagement, but when he starts making arrangements to send Mary Anne home, she disappears for three weeks into "that no-man's land between Cleveland Heights and deep jungle." When she returns, it is as one of the shadows that "float across the surface of the earth, like spirits, vaporous and unreal," disappearing into the Special Forces hootch. No longer a "social animal," she is "lost" forever to Mark and his control, passing over to the other side where hypermasculinity merges with the mysterious jungle.

Mark becomes emasculated in inverse proportion to Mary Anne's increasing autonomy, as if her transformation deprives him of his own traditional eighteen-year-old initiation into manhood. He makes a final stand one day outside the Special Forces area, telling Rat he'll "bring her out." By nightfall, "Fossie's face was slick with sweat. He looked sick. His eyes were bloodshot; his skin had a whitish, almost colorless cast." At midnight, Rat and Eddie Diamond find "the kid" transfixed by a weird music "like the noise of nature" accompanied by "a woman's voice ... half singing, half chanting .... the lyrics seemed to be in a foreign tongue" (118). The three men enter the hooch and find Mary Anne surrounded by accoutrements of dark pagan worship: candles, tribal music with "a weird deep-wilderness sound," and a "stench ... thick and numbing, like an animal's den, a mix of blood and scorched hair and excrement and the sweet-sour odor of moldering flesh—the stink of the kill." In one corner impaled on a post is "the decayed head of a large black leopard." Everywhere there are "stacks of bones—all kinds" and propped against a wall stands a poster: "ASSEMBLE YOUR OWN GOOK!! FREE SAMPLE KIT!!" This scene invites comparison with Coppola's almost camp representation of Kurtz's jungle compound, and one is not sure whether to laugh at the special effects or take them as serious depictions of transgression. In any event, when the men find Mary Anne, it is clear that her change is complete. Not only is she no longer feminine, but she is no longer human, as if a woman "perfectly at peace with herself" is no "person" at all, or no one the men can recognize: "It took a few seconds, Rat said, to appreciate the full change. In part it was her eyes: utterly flat and indifferent. There was no emotion in her stare, no sense of the person behind it. But the grotesque part, he said, was her jewelry. At the girl's throat was a necklace of human tongues. Elongated and narrow, like pieces of blackened leather, the tongues were threaded along a length of copper wire, one overlapping the next, the tips curled upward as if caught in a final shrill syllable" (120).

The necklace of tongues conveys multiple meanings. It is linked with other references to Mary Anne's entry to another language outside patriarchy: "a foreign tongue," "a woman's voice rising up in a language beyond translation." It is clearly part of the animal, natural world, beyond social order. Like Medusa's snakes, the necklace emphasizes an enforcing, stony silence. Mary Anne literally wears her own "gook" parts on her body, an image reminiscent of the more common string of ears collected as souvenirs by soldiers in many Vietnam war stories but more horrific, because they are decoratively flaunted. Tongues carry a multiplicitous sexual charge, suggesting both male and female genitalia, hetero- and homoerotic sexually. Her power is a particularly feminized form of monstrousness, a form of "jewelry" both alluring and threatening to castrate Mark's "solid brass balls." Once the men realize Mary Anne has transgressed the bounds of patriarchal propriety and order, "there was nothing to be done." They leave her in her lair, but not before she is granted one soliloquy that in fact explains nothing to the men except her absolute inscrutability and animalism, the voracious death-loving maw she has become. To the reader—particularly the female reader—the passage inverts the book's repeated pattern of blaming women for not understanding the war; here, the woman knows more than the men, and knowing is essentialized in terms of the female body:

'You just don't *know*' she said. 'You hide in this little fortress, behind wire and sandbags, and you don't know what it's all about. Sometimes I want to *eat* this place. Vietnam. I want to swallow the whole country—the dirt, the death—I just want to eat it and have it there inside me. That's how I feel. It's like ... this appetite. I get scared sometimes—lots of times—but it's not *bad*. You know? I feel close to myself. When I'm out there at night, I feel close to my own body, I can feel my blood moving, my skin and my fingernails, everything, it's like I'm full of electricity and I'm glowing in the dark—I'm on fire almost—I'm burning away into nothing—but it doesn't matter because I know exactly who I am. You can't feel like that anywhere else.' (121)

Indeed, Mary Anne has entered the only place where female language, autonomy, sexuality, and power make sense—beyond culture into an untranslatable heart of darkness and horror. If a reading of the story stopped here, it might appear to be a feminist assertion of semiotic power disrupting patriarchal symbolic order, a deconstruction of the myths of the American sweetheart and the American Dream suggesting that we are all complicit in the fall from innocence into the "Garden of Evil" that is Vietnam. O'Brien sounds theoretically sophisticated in such a passage, as if he's read plenty of French feminism. Rat himself sounds like a protofeminist in his commentary, once again appearing to erase gender difference while in fact emphasizing it: "She was a girl, that's all. I mean, if it was a guy, everybody'd say Hey, no big deal, he got caught up in the Nam shit, he got seduced by the Greenies. See what I mean? You got these blinders on about women. How gentle and peaceful they are. All that crap about how if we had a pussy for president there wouldn't be no more wars. Pure garbage. You got to get rid of that sexist attitude" (117). Aside from Rat's use of sexist language to critique sexism, it is important to note two things. First, Mary Anne's subjectivity, although given brief voice in the preceding passage, is never fully imagined. She is given no motive for her change and exists to register the men's reactions to her—both in the original story and in its retelling by both Rat and the narrator. Ultimately, what we understand about her is that the men do not understand her. Second, she ends up outside the social order altogether, "glowing in the dark" but also "burning away into nothing," her power unassimilated and ineffective: "And then one morning Mary Anne walked off into the mountains and did not come back." Unlike Coppola's Kurtz and Oliver Stone's Barnes in *Platoon*, ritualistically sacrificed because of their transgressions, she disappears into a disembodied spook story: "If you believed the Greenies, Rat said, Mary Anne was still somewhere out there in the dark ... She had crossed to the other side. She was part of the land. She was wearing her culottes, her pink sweater, and a necklace of human tongues. She was dangerous, She was ready for the kill" (125). O'Brien cannot imagine an ending for such a story; Mary

Anne is never elevated to the level of tragic heroine, but remains a sort of macabre, B-movie "joke," good for a nervous laugh among the men. Ultimately, her change changes nothing.

In the end, social order is restored and male homosocial bonds are re-established, exchanged—according to Sedgwick's paradigm—through the medium of Mary Anne's story. Even the segregated medics and the Greenies come together, because the final installment of Mary Anne's story is passed from one of the Greenies and Eddie Diamond to Rat Kiley to the Tim O'Brien narrator. Through storytelling, the men close ranks and banish the woman beyond the periphery of civilization. Having appropriated masculine power within a female body, she is seen as "dangerous" to the social order and becomes "part of the land." The men are allowed to maintain their image of the war-making female as an aberration from the norm, but Mary Anne is denied the freedom or power to tell her own story. Unlike the ending of *Apocalypse Now*, where Kurtz's embrace of "the horror" brings about either total chaos or cathartic purgation (depending on which version you see), Mary Anne's savagery and monstrousness function to solidify male bonds and validate the humanity of the more "normal" soldiers. She carries to the furthest extreme the book's pattern of excluding women from the storytelling circle.

VI

In the story that closes the book, "The Lives of the Dead," O'Brien makes a turn toward wholeness, closure, and regeneration. Here, for once, the feminine occupies a position in the same precious realm of the imagination as the masculine, although alternating sections again keep the war stories, the childhood stories, and the present-day metafictional commentary separate. The imagination, which was so dangerously distracting in "The Things They Carried," is now a force that keeps the dead alive and integrates the self by mixing memory and desire, "bringing body and soul back together," unifying through the shaping force of language and narrative form, "a little kid, twenty-three-year-old infantry sergeant, a middle-aged writer knowing guilt and sorrow"

(265). The narrator alternates in this story two primal experiences of death: his view of a Vietcong corpse on his fourth day in Vietnam, and his experience of love and loss at age nine. The story resurrects Linda, his fourth grade sweetheart, who died of a brain tumor. In retrospect, he imagines their first love as "pure knowing," imbued with the knowledge that "beyond language ... we were sharing something huge and permanent" (259). At this point in the book, the concept of merging wholly with another through "pure knowing" has accumulated the weight of fear (Jimmy Cross and Martha) and danger (Mary Anne and the war), both of which are also associated with transgressing normal gender codes and dissolving the socially constructed self. Here, the impulse seems to be to idealize youthful passion, distinguishing it from more frightening forms of grown-up "knowing." The narrator remembers that, in fact, his urge to tell stories has always been connected with resuscitating the dead. Grieving after Linda's death, he dreams of Linda coming back to comfort him: "Timmy, stop crying. It doesn't *matter.*" In the months following, he begins to make up elaborate stories to bring Linda alive and call her into his dreams. He writes the stories down and in their vividness they become real. He gives Linda a voice (which of course is only his own dream voice, the feminine within himself) and imagines her expressing herself with a literary metaphor, once more reinforcing the connection between gender and writing/storytelling, with the female figured as absence: "'Well, right now,' she said, 'I'm *not* dead. But when I am, it's like ... I don't know, I guess it's like being inside a book that nobody's reading.'" The strategy stuck with him, for "In Vietnam, too, we had ways of making the dead seem not quite so dead." The most important way, the book makes clear, is to both read and write the dead by telling stories woven "in the spell of memory and imagination."

"The Lives of the Dead" reverses the book's opening story, "The Things They Carried," for here the imagination, linked with the memory of a girl, is not a dangerous force but is redemptive and regenerative. The story also moves beyond the antagonistic polarity of gender that marks the other *Esquire* stories. Linda is forever innocent and forever young, an idealized Laura or Beatrice or Annabel Lee who comes when bidden as muse for the narrator's cathartic stories. Although it sounds ungenerous to critique such a moving and lovely story, one must wonder whether the book's only positive and unthreatening representation of femininity is possible because she is forever pre-pubescent, safely encased in memory, dream, death, and narrative. Unlike Martha or Mary Anne or Curt Lemon's sister, she never grows up to be a castrating "cooze" or savage monster. She never touches the war, thus never intrudes upon his homosocial bonds; rather, the narrator uses her, as male writers have always used female muses, to find his voice and arrive at his own understanding of his traumas. In the context of all the other war stories in the book, Linda still functions as part of a triangle; she is the mediator that facilitates the narrator's reconciliation with his own past in Vietnam and his recovery of a whole self. It is tempting to read that self as universally human, but the force of the whole preceding book cautions us that it is a masculine self wounded in war and recovered in war stories. Woman can only play dead or absent muse to the central masculine subject.

The Things They Carried contributes significantly to the canon of Vietnam War fiction. It is a remarkable treatment of the epistemology of writing and the psychology of soldiering. It dismantles many stereotypes that have dominated Hollywood treatments of the Vietnam War and distorted our understanding: the basket-case veteran (the book's narrator is reasonably well-adjusted), the macho war lover (characters such as Azar are presented as extreme aberrations), the callous officer (Jimmy Cross is fallible and sympathetic), the soldier as victim of government machinations, the peace movement, or apathetic civilians. The book probes the vulnerability of soldiers betrayed by cultural myths and registers how deeply war in our culture is a gendered activity. But O'Brien inscribes no critique of his characters' misogyny or the artificial binary opposition of masculinity and femininity, no redefinition of power, no fissure in the patriarchal discourse of war. However ambiguous and horrible Vietnam may be, and however many new combinations of memory, fact, and imagination O'Brien composes, war is still presented as an inevitable, natural phenomenon deeply meaningful to the male psyche and hostile to femininity. More pernicious, these stories seem to warn women readers away from any empathetic grasp of "the things men do."

STEVEN KAPLAN ON THE UNDYING UNCERTAINTY OF THE NARRATOR

Conveying the average soldier's sense of uncertainty about what actually happened in Vietnam by presenting the what-ifs and maybes as if they were facts, and then calling these facts back into question again, can be seen as a variation of the haunting phrase used so often by American soldiers to convey their own uncertainty about what happened in Vietnam: "there it is." They used it to make the unspeakable and indescribable and the uncertain real and present for a fleeting moment. Similarly, O'Brien presents facts and stories that are only temporarily certain and real; the strange "balance" in Vietnam between "crazy and almost crazy" (20) always creeps back in and forces the mind that is remembering and retelling a story to remember and retell it one more time in a different form, adding different nuances, and then to tell it again one more time.

Storytelling in this book is something in which "the whole world is rearranged" (39) in an effort to get at the "full truth" (49) about events that themselves deny the possibility of arriving at something called the "full", meaning certain and fixed, "truth." By giving the reader facts and then calling those facts into question, by telling stories and then saying that those stories happened (147), and then that they did not happen (203), and then that they might have happened (204), O'Brien puts more emphasis in *The Things They Carried* on the question that he first posed in *Going After Cacciato*: how can a work of fiction become paradoxically more real than the events upon which it is based, and how can the confusing experiences of the average soldier in Vietnam be conveyed in such a way that they will acquire at least a momentary sense of certainty. In *The Things They Carried*, this question is raised even before the novel begins. The book opens with a reminder: "This is a work of fiction. Except for a few details regarding the author's own life, all the incidents, names, and characters are imaginary." Two pages later we are told that "this book is lovingly dedicated to the men of Alpha Company, and in particular to Jimmy Cross, Norman Bowker, Rat Kiley, Mitchell Sanders, Henry Dobbins, and Kiowa." We discover only a few pages after this dedication that those six men are the novel's main characters.

These prefatory comments force us simultaneously to consider the unreal (the fictions that follow) as real because the book is dedicated to the characters who appear in it, and the "incidents, names, and characters" are unreal or "imaginary." O'Brien informs us at one point that in telling these war stories he intends to get at the "full truth" (49) about them; yet from the outset he has shown us that the full truth as he sees it is in itself something ambiguous. Are these stories and the characters in them real or imaginary, or does the "truth" hover somewhere between the two? A closer look at the book's narrative structure reveals that O'Brien is incapable of answering the questions that he initially raises, because the very act of writing fiction about the war, of telling war stories. as he practices it in *The Things They Carried*, is determined by the nature of the Vietnam War and ultimately by life in general where "the only certainty is overwhelming ambiguity" (88).

The emphasis on ambiguity behind auburns narrative technique in *The Things They Carried* is thus similar to the pattern used by Joseph Conrad's narrator, Marlow, in *Heart of Darkness*, so incisively characterized by J. Hillis Miller as a lifting of veils to reveal a truth that is quickly obscured again by the dropping of a new veil (158). Over and over again, O'Brien tells us that we are reading "the full and exact truth" (181), and yet, as we make our way through this book and gradually find the same stories being retold with new facts and from a new perspective. we come to realize that there is no such thing as the full and exact truth. Instead. the only thing that can be determined at the end of the story is its own indeterminacy.

O'Brien calls telling stories in this manner "Good Form" in the title of one of the chapters of *The Things They Carried*: This is good form because "telling stories" like this "can make things present" (204). The stories in this book are not truer than the actual things that happened in Vietnam because they contain some higher, metaphysical truth: "True war stones do not generalize. They do not indulge in abstractions or analysis" (84). Rather, these stories are true because the characters and events within them are being given a new life each time they are told and retold. This approach to storytelling echoes Wolfgang Iser's theory of representation in his essay "Representation: A Performative Act":

Whatever shape or form these various (philosophical or fictional) conceptualizations (of life) may have, their common denominator is the attempt to explain origins. In this respect they close off those very potentialities that literature holds open. Of course literature also springs from the same anthropological need, since it stages what is inaccessible, thus compensating for the impossibility of knowing what it is to be. But literature is not an explanation of origins; it is a staging of the constant deferment of explanation, which makes the origin explode into its multifariousness.

It is at this point that aesthetic semblance makes its full impact. Representation arises out of and thus entails the removal of difference, whose irremovability transforms representation into a performative act of staging something. This staging is almost infinitely variable, for in contrast to explanations, no single staging could ever remove difference and so explain origin. on the contrary, its very multiplicity facilitates an unending mirroring of what man is, because no mirrored manifestation can ever coincide with our actual being. (245)

When we conceptualize life, we attempt to step outside

ourselves and look at who we are. We constantly make new attempts to conceptualize our lives and uncover our true identities because looking at who we might be is as close as we can come to discovering who we actually are. Similarly, representing events in fiction is an attempt to understand them by detaching them from the "real world" and placing them in a world that is being staged. In *The Things They Carried*, Tim O'Brien desperately struggles to make his readers believe that what they are reading is true because he wants them to step outside their everyday reality and participate in the events that he is portraying: he wants us to believe in his stories to the point where we are virtually in the stories so that we might gain a more thorough understanding of, or feeling for, what is being portrayed in them. Representation as O'Brien practices it in this book is not a mimetic act but a "game," as Iser also calls it in a more recent essay, "The Play of the Text," a process of acting things out:

> Now since the latter (the text) is fictional, it automatically invokes a convention-governed contract between author and reader indicating that the textual world is to be viewed not as reality but as if it *were* reality. And so whatever is repeated in the text is not meant to denote the world, but merely a world enacted. This may well repeat an identifiable reality, but it contains one all-important difference: what happens within it is relieved of the consequences inherent in the real world referred to. Hence in disclosing itself, fictionality signalizes that everything is only to be taken *as if* it were what it seems to be, to be taken—in other words—as play. (251)

In *The Things They Carried*, representation includes staging what might have happened in Vietnam while simultaneously questioning the accuracy and credibility of the narrative act itself. The reader is thus made fully aware of being made a participant in a game, in a "performative act," and thereby also is asked to become immediately involved in the incredibly frustrating act of trying to make sense of events that resist understanding. The reader is permitted to experience at first hand the uncertainty that characterized being in Vietnam. We are being forced to "believe" (79) that the only "certainty" was the "overwhelming ambiguity."

This process is nowhere clearer than in a chapter appropriately called "How to Tell A True War Story." O'Brien opens this chapter by telling us "THIS IS TRUE." Then he takes us through a series of variations of the story about how Curt Lemon stepped on a mine and was blown up into a tree. The only thing true or certain about the story, however, is that it is being constructed and then deconstructed and then reconstructed right in front of us. The reader is given six different versions of the death of Curt Lemon, and each version is so discomforting that it is difficult to come up with a more accurate statement to describe his senseless death than "there it is." Or as O'Brien puts it—"in the end, really there's nothing much to say about a true war story, except maybe 'oh'" (84).

Before we learn in this chapter how Curt Lemon was killed, we are told the "true" story that Rat Kiley apparently told to the character-narrator O'Brien about how Kiley wrote to Lemon's sister and "says he loved the guy. He says the guy was his best friend in the world" (76). Two months after writing the letter, Kiley has not heard from Lemon's sister, and so he writes her off as a "dumb cooze" (76). This is what happened according to Kiley, and O'Brien assures us that the story is "incredibly sad and true" (77). However, when Rat Kiley tells a story in another chapter we are warned that he

swore up and down to its truth, although in the end, I'll admit, that doesn't amount to much of a warranty. Among the men in Alpha Company, Rat had a reputation for exaggeration and overstatement, a compulsion to rev up the facts, and for most of us it was normal procedure to discount sixty or seventy percent of anything he had to say. (101)

Rat Kiley is an unreliable narrator, and his facts are always distorted, but this does not affect storytelling truth as far as

O'Brien is concerned. The passage above on Rat Kiley's credibility as a storyteller concludes: "It wasn't a question of deceit. Just the opposite: he wanted to heat up the truth, to make it burn so hot that you would feel exactly what he felt" (101). This summarizes O'Brien's often confusing narrative strategy in *The Things They Carried*: the facts about what actually happened, or whether anything happened at all, are not important. They cannot be important because they themselves are too uncertain, too lost in a world in which certainty had vanished somewhere between the "crazy and almost crazy." The important thing is that any story about the war, any "true war story," must "burn so hot" when it is told that it becomes alive for the listener-reader in the act of its telling.

In Rat Kiley's story about how he wrote to Kurt Lemon's sister, the details we are initially given are exaggerated to the point where, in keeping with O'Brien's fire metaphor, they begin to heat up. Kurt Lemon, we are told, "would always volunteer for stuff nobody else would volunteer for in a million years" (75). And once Lemon went fishing with a crate of hand grenades, "the funniest thing in world history ... about twenty zillion dead gook fish" (76). But the story does not get so hot that it burns, it does not become so "incredibly sad and true," as O'Brien puts it, until we find out at the story's close that, in Rat's own words, "I write this beautiful fuckin letter, I slave over it, and what happens? The dumb cooze never writes back" (77). It is these words and not the facts that come before them that make the story true for O'Brien.

At the beginning of this chapter, O'Brien asks us several times to "Listen to Rat," to listen how he says things more than to what he says. And of all of the words that stand out in his story, it is the word "cooze" (which is repeated four times in two pages), that makes his story come alive for O'Brien. "You can tell a true war story by its absolute and uncompromising allegiance to obscenity and evil" (76). This is just one way that O'Brien gives for determining what constitutes a true war story. The unending list of possibilities includes reacting to a story with the ambiguous words "Oh" and "There it is." Rat Kiley's use of "cooze" is another in the sequence of attempts to utter some truth about the Vietnam experience and, by extension. about war in general. There is no moral to be derived from this word such as war is obscene or corrupt: "A true war story is never moral. It does not instruct" (76). There is simply the real and true fact that the closest thing to certainty and truth in a war story is a vague utterance, a punch at the darkness, an attempt to rip momentarily through the veil that repeatedly recovers the reality and truth of what actually happened.

It is thus probably no coincidence that in the middle of this chapter on writing a true war story, O'Brien tells us that "Even now, at this instant," Mitchell Sanders's "yo-yo" is the main thing he can remember from the short time encompassing Lemon's death (83). This object, associated with games and play, becomes a metaphor for the playful act of narration that O'Brien practices in this book, a game that he plays by necessity. The only way to tell a true war story, according to O'Brien, is to keep telling it "one more time, patiently, adding and subtracting, making up a few things to get at the real truth" (91), which ultimately is impossible because the real truth, the full truth, as the events themselves, are lost forever in "a great ghostly fog, thick and permanent" (88). You only "tell a true war story" "if you just keep on telling it" (91) because "absolute occurrence is irrelevant" (89). The truth, then, is clearly not something that can be distinguished or separated from the storm itself, and the reality or non-reality of the story's events is not something that can be determined from a perspective outside of the story. As the critic Geoffrey Hartman says about poetry: "To keep a poem in mind is to keep it there, not to resolve it into available meanings" (274). Similarly, for O'Brien it is not the fact that a story happened that makes it true and worth remembering, anymore than the story itself can be said to contain a final truth. The important thing is that a story becomes so much a part of the present that "there is nothing to remember (while we are reading it) except the story" (40). This is why O'Brien's narrator is condemned, perhaps in a positive sense, to telling and then retelling numerous variations of the same story over and over and over again. This is also why he introduces each new version of a story with such comments as:

"This one does it for me. I have told it before many times, many versions—but here is what actually happened" (85). What actually happened, the story's truth, can only become apparent for the fleeting moment in which it is being told; that truth will vanish back into the fog just as quickly as the events that occurred in Vietnam were sucked into a realm of uncertainty the moment they occurred.

O'Brien demonstrates nothing new about trying to tell war stories—that the "truths" they contain "are contradictory" (87), elusive, and thus indeterminate. Two hundred years ago, Goethe, as he tried to depict the senseless bloodshed during the allied invasion of revolutionary France, also reflected in his autobiographical essay *Campaign in France* on the same inevitable contradictions that arise when one speaks of what happened or might have happened in battle. Homer's *Iliad* is, of course, the ultimate statement on the contradictions inherent in war. However, what is new in O'Brien's approach in *The Things They Carried* is that he makes the axiom that in war "almost everything is true. Almost nothing is true" (87) the basis for the act of telling a war story.

The narrative strategy that O'Brien uses in this book to portray the uncertainty of what happened in Vietnam is not restricted to depicting war, and O'Brien does not limit it to the war alone. He concludes his book with a chapter titled "The Lives of the Dead" in which he moves from his experiences in Vietnam back to when he was nine years old. On the surface, the book's last chapter is about O'Brien's first date, his first love, a girl named Linda who died of a brain tumor a few months after he had taken her to see the movie, *The Man Who Never Was*. What this chapter is really about, however, as its title suggests, is how the dead (which also include people who may never have actually existed) can be given life in a work of fiction. In a story, O'Brien tells us, "memory and imagination and language combine to make spirits in the head. There is the illusion of aliveness" (260). Like the man who never was in the film of that title, the people that never were except in memories and the imagination can become real or alive, if only for a moment, through the act of storytelling.

According to O'Brien, when you tell a story, really tell it, "you objectify your own experience. You separate it from yourself" (178). By doing this you are able to externalize "a swirl of memories that might otherwise have ended in paralysis or worse" (179). However, the storyteller does not just escape from the events and people in a story by placing them on paper; as we have seen, the act of telling a given story is an ongoing and never-ending process. By constantly involving and then re-involving the reader in the task of determining what "actually" happened in a given situation, in a story, and by forcing the reader to experience the impossibility of ever knowing with any certainty what actually happened, O'Brien liberates himself from the lonesome responsibility of remembering and trying to understand events. He also creates a community of individuals immersed in the act of experiencing the uncertainty or indeterminacy of all events, regardless of whether they occurred in Vietnam, in a small town in Minnesota (253–273), or somewhere in the reader's own life.

O'Brien thus saves himself, as he puts it in the last sentence of his book, from the fate of his character Norman Bowker who, in a chapter called "Speaking of Courage," kills himself because he cannot find some lasting meaning in the horrible things he experienced in Vietnam. O'Brien saves himself by demonstrating in this book that the most important thing is to be able to recognize and accept that events have no fixed or final meaning and that the only meaning that events can have is one that emerges momentarily and then shifts and changes each time that the events come alive as they are remembered or portrayed.

The character Norman Bowker hangs himself in the locker room of the local YMCA after playing basketball with some friends (181), partially because he has a story locked up inside of himself that he feels he cannot tell because no one would want to hear it. It is the story of how he failed to save his friend, Kiowa,[2] from drowning in a field of human excrement: "A good war story, he thought, but it was not a war for war stories, not for talk of valor, and nobody in town wanted to know about the stink. They wanted good intentions and good deeds" (169). Bowker's dilemma is remarkably similar to that of Krebs in Hemingway's story "Soldier's Home": "At first Krebs ... did not want to talk about the war at all. Later he felt the need to talk but no one wanted to hear about it. His town had heard too many atrocity stones to be thrilled by actualities" (Hemingway 145).

O'Brien, after his war, took on the task "of grabbing people by the shirt and explaining exactly what had happened to me" (179). He explains in *The Things They Carried* that it is impossible to know "exactly what had happened." He wants us to know all of the things he/they/we did not know about Vietnam and will probably never know. He wants us to feel the sense of uncertainty that his character/narrator Tim O'Brien experiences twenty years after the war when he returns to the place where his friend Kiowa sank into a "field of shit" and tries to find "something meaningful and right" (212) to say but ultimately can only say, "well ... there it is" (212). Each time we, the readers of *The Things They Carried*, return to Vietnam through O'Brien's labyrinth of stories, we become more and more aware that this statement is the closest we probably ever will come to knowing the "real truth," the undying uncertainty of the Vietnam War.

Note
2. In the "Notes" to this chapter, O'Brien typically turns the whole story upside down "in the interest of truth" and tells us that Norman Bowker was not responsible for Kiowa's horrible death: "That part of the story is my own" (182). This phrase could be taken to mean that this part of the story is his own creation or that he was the one responsible for Kiowa's death.

MARILYN WESLEY ON TRUTH AND FICTION

Postmodern Morality in *The Things They Carried*
The title story of *The Things They Carried* invokes and revises two key devices of generic war fiction: the structure of dramatic action and the focal representation of the officer. Buried within

this narrative is a conventional plot. A platoon of infantrymen from Alpha Company, led by Lieutenant Jimmy Cross, is on a mission to destroy Viet Cong "villes" and tunnels. The seventeen men—among them, Ted Lavender, Lee Strunk, Rat Kiley, Henry Dobbins, Mitchell Sanders, Dave Jensen, Norman Bowker, Kiowa, and Tim O'Brien, characters who recur throughout the collection—are especially uneasy when they discover a tunnel. Standard operating procedure demands that one of their number, chosen by lot, crawl inside and explore before they blow it up, a maneuver literally dangerous and psychologically unnerving. On the day of the story, Lee Strunk is unlucky enough to have to descend. The others, worried for him and uneasily aware of their own mortality, await his eventual reemergence. Although Strunk returns unscathed, Ted Lavender, the most frightened of the group, is later shot while urinating. A helicopter is summoned to remove his body, and the men respond to his death in a variety of ways: relief, humor, hysterical grief, and the destruction of the nearby village of Than Khe.

This imposed dramatic structure of violation and resolution, which makes violent death and chaotic response comprehensible, is not adapted by the story, which is, instead, organized as lists of actual and emotional burdens toted by the soldiers. The things they carry include the accouterments of war, such as steel helmets, which, O'Brien carefully notes, weigh 5 pounds; the particular objects of their military duties, the 23-pound M-60 of the machine gunner or the medic's bag of "morphine and plasma and malaria tablets and surgical tape and comic books ... for a total weight of almost 20 pounds" (1990, 6–7); and the heavier load of fear and whatever the men rely on to cope with fear, like Ted Lavender's drugs, Kiowa's bible, and Jimmy Cross's love letters.

In *Writing War* Hanley contends that modern military narratives are suffused with a "'secret unacknowledged elation' at the thought of war, with the conviction that tear is exciting,"[2] and that this style of representation has promoted war as a desirable societal event (1991, 4). But by presenting violence in terms of burden rather than battle through deliberately non-dramatic structure, by stressing the continuous pressure of war rather than the climactic action of combat through the metaphor of weight to be borne, "The Things They Carried" deflates the excitement of traditional portrayal of the violence of the military adventure, and it deflects the ascription of moral purpose to the violent events of war.

Similarly, this story, which foregrounds the reactions of Lieutenant Jimmy Cross, obviates his reception as noble example. Jimmy fights the inexpressible fear the men share by obsessing about a girl he wants to love and substituting the banalities of her letters for the reality of Vietnam. After Lavender's death, Cross digs a foxhole and gives in to uncontrolled weeping. Finally, despite the rain, he burns the letters. Accepting the "blame" for his soldier's death, he resolves to be a leader, not a lover, "determined to perform his duties firmly and without negligence" (O'Brien 1990, 24). He imagines himself, henceforth, an officer in the manner of John Wayne: "if anyone quarreled or complained, he would simply tighten his lips and arrange his shoulders in the correct command posture.... He might just shrug and say, Carry on, then they would saddle up and form into a column and move on ..." (1990, 25). Like the rest of the men, the lieutenant responds to the random violence in largely unproductive ways. He doesn't set any superior standard because, like the others, he can find no relevant standard to set.

Of course, Lavender's death cannot be explained or contained by Cross's pose of heroic responsibility any more than it can be relieved by the unit's destruction of the "chickens and dogs" and hootches of Than Khe (O'Brien 1990, 16). In "The Things They Carried," the unplottable violence of the Vietnam experience is structurally contrasted to the assimilable violence of war as popular fiction. In the space between these two opposed representations—experiential disorder, the way the events of war feel to the soldiers in the field, and fictive order, the way popular representations suggest they should respond—emerges the "truth" about Vietnam as a constant process of "humping" or carrying the impossible responsibility of power through a violent landscape.

The proper treatment of this truth, O'Brien suggests, is storytelling. Conditioned as we are to the designations of "fiction" and "non-fiction," it is easy to imagine that truth and stories are opposite categories. "How to Tell a True War Story," however, dissolves this relation to allow storytelling to emerge as the pursuit of provisional comprehension. Two scenes of graphic violence organize this effect. The first is the death of a young soldier who steps on a mine during a happy moment; the second is the destruction of a baby water buffalo by his best friend:

1. In the mountains that day, I watched Lemon turn sideways. He laughed and said something to Rat Kiley. Then he took a peculiar half-step, moving from the shade into bright sunlight, and the booby-trapped 105 round blew him into a tree. The parts were just hanging there, so Dave Jensen and I were ordered to shinny up and peel him off. I remember pieces of skin and something wet and yellow that must've been the intestines. The gore was horrible, and stays with me. (O'Brien 1990, 89)

2. He stepped back and shot it through the front right knee. The animal did not make a sound. It went down hard, then got up again and Rat took careful aim and shot off an ear. He shot it in the hindquarters and in the little hump at its back. It wasn't to kill; it was to hurt. He put the rifle muzzle up against the mouth and shot the mouth away. Nobody said much. The whole platoon stood there feeling all sorts of things, but there wasn't a great deal of pity for the water buffalo. (O'Brien 1990, 86)

The passage continues in this vein. Rat shoots off the tail, then wounds the baby water buffalo in the ribs, the belly, the knee, the nose, and the throat. It is still living when one of the men kicks it, and the group finally dumps it into the village well.

It is impossible to read these two passages without placing them in a causal relationship that induces emotional and political interpretation. The juxtaposition of nature and death is especially shocking. In the first scene the sunlit American boy is wastefully decimated by a hidden explosive device. Rat Kiley and Curt Lemon have just been playing catch with a smoke bomb, turning war, for a few moments of pastoral innocence, into a carefree game.[3] But the Vietnamese have, evidently, broken the rules. An invisible enemy, they not only kill Curt, but cruelly dismember him. Although presented as a kind of hero, Curt is reduced to a substance to be peeled off and scraped away. A similar ironic reversal, Curt's "wet" and "yellow" intestines are converted from organs of life to signifiers of death.

The second scene is, apparently, a direct result of the first. Rat chooses a symbol of Vietnamese innocence, the ubiquitous water buffalo, which is an emblem of the culture, not an agent of war, and a "baby" at that, to mimic Curt, who has been cast as the momentary emblem of youthful American guilelessness. The horrific attack on the body of the animal mimics his friend's fragmentation and evisceration. The biblical motto of vengeance, "an eye for an eye ...," is literally enacted in a narrative sequence meant to inscribe the sense of just retribution. Revenge, as David Whillock notes, is a common plot device in film treatments of the Vietnam war which attempt to impose the closure "that was not possible" in actuality (1990, 310). This text, however, will not let the imputed causal attributions stand. At the end of the account of Curt Lemon's death, O'Brien appends a narrative interpolation: "But what wakes me up twenty years later is Dave Jensen singing 'Lemon Tree' as we threw down the parts" (1990, 89). Dave's humor, probably a means of self-protection, nevertheless deflects an automatic assignment of blame. Similarly, previous details about some of Curt's playful "pranks" disrupt his reception as an innocent character. In the condoling letter Rat writes to Curt's sister he describes a terrifying incident he thinks of as funny: "On Halloween night, this hot spooky night, the dude paints up his body all different colors and puts on this weird mask and hikes over to a ville and goes trick-or-treating almost stark naked, just boots and balls and an M-16" (76).

124

As a conclusion to the description of Rat's actions, O'Brien condenses the general reaction of the men into another gnomic comment by Jensen: "'Amazing,' Dave Jensen kept saying. 'A new wrinkle. I never seen it before'" (1990, 86). The awful humor of Jensen's song and his appreciative acknowledgement of the peculiar novelty of Rat's performance both undercut the causal efficacy of the sequence, which is, in fact, denied sequentiality by its placement within a fiction organized as an essay on writing the war story. And even while reacting with shock and sadness to the extensive catalogue of assaults on the body parts of the baby water buffalo, a reader may respond with irreverence to the exaggeration of the attenuated murder, an unwilling recognition of the kind of overstatement that signals a gag rather than a tragedy. This subversion of narrative causality is further reinforced as O'Brien alternates accounts of action with lectures on the postmodern tests of a "true war story" "How to Tell ..." exemplifies: it cannot moralize or generalize, it will probably be obscene and most certainly embarrassing, and it will overturn convictions by muddling oppositional categories of truth and fiction, good and evil, and love and war (77, 84, 89, 90). The effect of the true war story will be to replace certainty with confusion.

Notes

2. The quotation Hanley cites comes from Doris Lessing's *Prisons We Choose to Live Inside* (1987), in which Lessing argues for the open acknowledgement of the pleasurable excitement with which many people respond to the activities of war.

3. Fussell notes the constant trope of the game in World War I. Not only did writers compare battles to football, regiments were encouraged into battle by leaders who supplied balls to kick into enemy territory. "Modern mass wars," he explains, "require in their early stages a definitive work of popular literature demonstrating how much wholesome fun is to be had at the training camp" (1975, 18). O'Brien's invocation of this war-as-the-play-of-boys metaphor reverses the assumptions that war, like games, is bound by rules, that winning is what is important, and that the uncomplicated companionship of young males is an important result of military experience.

David R. Jarraway on Trauma and Recovery in Vietnam War Literature

War becomes the equivalent of human waste—"a goddamn shit field" (*Things* 164)—in which an entire platoon must immerse itself in order to register most completely the nauseous vacuity and repulsive futility of their lives at war: "[A]fter a few days, the Song Tra Bong overflowed its banks and the land turned into a deep, thick muck for a half mile on either side.... Like quicksand, almost, except the stink was incredible.... You'd just sink in. You'd feel it ooze up over your body and sort of suck you down.... I mean, it never stopped, not ever" (161). "Finally somebody figured it out. What this was, it was.... The village toilet. No indoor plumbing, right? So they used the field" (164). "Rain and slop and shrapnel, it all mixed together, and the field seemed to boil ... with the waste and the war" (191). "For twenty years," O'Brien's novel's narrator later remarks in hindsight, "this field had embodied all the waste that was Vietnam, all the vulgarity and horror" (210). That the full impact, however, of the "excremental assault" of my title should come to be realized so belatedly—*In Retrospect*, as Robert McNamara most recently puts forward the case—is, ironically, Vietnam's most extravagantly wasteful legacy.[1] But as one of O'Brien's least savory platoon members is given to remark, "'Eating shit—it's your classic irony'" (187).

Irony is the trope of trash or waste. And while it's not central to my purpose to trash or waste some of the more well-known literary theories endeavoring to come to terms with, if not indeed aiming to recover from, that extraordinarily riddling concatenation of events that is "Vietnam," I nonetheless want to cultivate a healthy sense of irony in an effort to disclose what discursive representations of war—theoretical as well as artistic—may actually be endeavoring to cover over or cover up—to re-cover, as it were.[2] The fiction of Tim O'Brien, *The Things They Carried* in particular, with its own healthy sense of irony, can gesture toward the shortcomings of theory. But, as I shall argue later, in keeping with that penetrating sense of irony even some of the best insights of this work may, too, have gone to waste, driving us on to O'Brien's next and most recent novel, *In the Lake of the Woods* (1994).

Kali Tal, in her important essay "Speaking the Language of Pain," has been in the vanguard of a number of important writers to locate Vietnam literature in the context of the discourse of trauma.[3] In so doing, Tal underscores the chief failing of most literary theorists attempting to deal holistically with the war, namely, "their inevitable and total reduction of the war to metaphor" (Tal 223), whether this be the war's likeness to the myth-making of classic American literature (Philip Beidler), to the psychic landscape in literature closer to the present (John Hellman), or to the construction of the American self-image in the literature of the future (Thomas Myers)[4] As with all experiences of trauma (Holocaust literature, rape literature, incest literature, etc.), according to Tal, "Reality so violates personal mythologies" that only the example of "the literal immersion of concentration camp victims in shit ... of being forced to wear, eat, or swim in excrement"—only such "excremental assault" (a phrase she borrows from Terrance Des Pres's *The Survivor: An Anatomy of Life in the Death Camps* [1976])—can approximate the individual's totally abject sense of psychic and social "violation" (Tal 234). Yet the transformation of national or cultural myths is dependent organically upon the revision of personal myths (Tal 243). Hence, any kind of real social or cultural amelioration envisioned in mythically discursive terms is most likely to occur as a consequence of trauma, whose excremental horror "strike[s] at the very core of the victim's conception of self in the world, forcing the most radical restructuring of personal myth ... to include the previously unthinkable" (234).[5]

What Tal, however, is insistent upon throughout her essay is the almost impossible task to which the trauma author becomes heir. "For if the goal is to convey the traumatic experience," as she explains, "no secondhand rendering of it is adequate. The horrific events which have reshaped the author's construction of reality can only be described [and] not re-created" (Tal 231). Thus, the trauma author appears forever to be laboring in a "liminal state," a kind of "unbridgeable gap between writer and reader" (218) that is bounded, on the one side, by "the urge to bear witness, to carry the tale of horror back to the halls of normalcy" (229), and on the other, by "the truth of the experience" that "in even the most powerful writing ... language cannot reach or explicate" (222). Working at cross-purposes in this way, the trauma author is rather like O'Brien's Lieutenant Jimmy Cross in *The Things They Carried*, never quite succeeding in having his men "get their shit together, ... keep it together, and maintain it neatly and in good working order" (*Things* 24).[6]

The closest experience, therefore, that we as readers of Vietnam literature are ever likely to have that might approximate something of its trauma will undoubtedly lie, along with its authors, in that "liminal state" between what we may already know too well, and what we sense is hardly there for us to imagine. The two senses of "re-covery" in my title noted previously thus speak to both sides of trauma's liminal divide. Georges Bataille, who perhaps knows more about excremental assault than most, in his *Visions of Excess* gives us the initial sense of a calculated recovery, usually in closed forms of discourse whose economy, in the end, "is limited to reproduction and to the conservation of human life" (116). In more open forms of discourse, however, whose economy of "unproductive expenditure" is likely to include the traumas of "war" and "perverse sexual activity" (118), we have the quite other sense of a more radical form of recovery since expenditure, as revealed in its "excremental symbolism," is mainly "directed toward loss" rather than "the principle of conservation" and the "stability of fortunes" (122).

Recovery from trauma, then, in this more radical form can only proceed, as Tal suggests, by way of a restructuring of personal experience in a wholly expendable way. In contrast, the more conservative notion of recovery, by falling back upon the already known and familiar, will negate the reality of trauma by failing to include in personal experience what has been formerly left unthought. And yet the temptation to collapse the former sense of recovery into the latter, in effect, to cover up the trauma that is Vietnam, would appear to be overwhelming, as that horror is strikingly rendered in *The Things They Carried*:

> For the common soldier, at least, war has the feel—the spiritual texture—of a great ghostly fog, thick and permanent. There is no clarity. Everything swirls. The old rules are no longer binding, the old truths no longer true. Right spills over into wrong. Order blends into chaos, love into hate, ugliness into beauty, law into anarchy, civility into savagery. The vapors suck you in. You can't tell where you are, or why you're there, and the only certainty is overwhelming ambiguity. In war you lose your sense of the definite, hence your sense of truth itself, and therefore it's safe to say that in a true war.story nothing is ever absolutely true. (88)

Nonetheless, O'Brien, like Bataille, will hew to that loss of the definite, and elsewhere insist on the war's "uncertainty" (*Things* 44), its "mystery" (209), and what he candidly admits is sometimes "just beyond telling" (79).[7] For if there is to be any kind of recovery from the trauma that promises no more Vietnams, only the kind of openness and responsiveness to experience that can make what is "absolutely true" quite expendable will do. In place of a character like Rat Kiley whose obsession with "policing up the parts" and "plugging up holes" (249–50) ultimately leads to his turning his own gun on himself as the sure fire method of withstanding change, O'Brien perhaps suggests something more redemptive in the example of an unknown soldier waist-deep back in the shit field: "Bent forward at the waist, groping with both hands, he seemed to be chasing some creature just beyond reach, something elusive, a fish or a frog" (192). Bataille, in a passage that elucidates O'Brien's description of the shit field, writes: "[T]he moment when the ordered and reserved ... lose themselves for ends that cannot be subordinated to anything one can account for" is precisely that moment when "life starts" (Bataille 128).

Life starts for both the authors and readers of Vietnam literature in those moments when the most authentic form of recovery in the trauma text represents a groping after the unaccountable, the unthinkable, and the unsayable. In the space remaining, I will dwell on three such exemplary moments in O'Brien's work—moments in which the excremental assault of war proves to be almost insupportable. In each case, nothing less than a wholly new conceptualization of subjectivity is called for—a "traumatic moment of epiphany," as it were (?i?ek 34). And the recovery's success will largely depend upon the degree to which, translating Tal in the terms of both Bataille and O'Brien, the radical restructuring of personal myth will be carried forward in the direction of "things" that cannot be subordinated to anything one can discursively account for.

My first examples of a promised recovery occurs, predictably enough, exactly at that moment, in the "Sweetheart of the Song Tra Bong" chapter of O'Brien's *Things*, when the character involved disappears at its end: "She [Mary Anne Bell] had crossed to the other side. She was part of the land.... She was dangerous. She was ready for the kill" (125). Mary Anne is the seventeen-year-old girlfriend of Mark Fossie whom he secretly flies from Cleveland to Vietnam to keep him company between battle maneuvers. Scandalously out of place in the battlefield, Mary Anne nonetheless is for a time tolerated by platoon members to the extent that she confirms their sexist myths of the active and aggressive male and the passive and docile female in cultures both home and abroad: "The way she looked, Mary Anne made you think about those girls back home, how clean and innocent they all are, how they'll never understand any of this, not in a billion years" (123).

But very quickly, Mary Anne becomes immersed in the excremental assault of war first hand—"She was up to her eyeballs in it," Rat Kiley acerbically remarks (*Things* 123)—and as a result, gradually begins to alter her sense of self by forming new attachments to the Green Berets, undertaking to assist medically in the fields of combat, and eventually embroiling herself directly in ambush operations, sometimes for weeks at a stretch. The "new confidence in her voice, [and] new authority in the ways she carried herself" (109), in the end, instructively reveals that the trauma of wartime liminality—"that mix of unnamed terror and unnamed pleasure" (123)[8]—can sometimes prove to have beneficial consequences, provided, as Rat Kiley ironically observes, that "you know you're risking something":

> [Y]ou become intimate with danger; you're in touch with the far side of yourself, as though it's another hemisphere, and you want to string it out and go wherever the trip takes you and be host to all the possibilities inside yourself. Not *bad*, she'd said. Vietnam made her glow in the dark. She wanted more, she wanted to penetrate deeper into the mystery of herself, and after a time the wanting became needing, which turned then to craving.... She was lost inside herself. (124)

In losing her self, echoing Bataille, to a host of possibilities not restricted in any sense to the essentializing exclusiveness of culturally approbated gender roles, trauma thus moves Mary Anne into that healthful space that "cannot be condensed into a 'proper locus,'" to borrow the phrasing of Elspeth Probyn, and where the self finds its recovery "as a theoretical manoeuvring, not as a unifying principle" (106). And if Mary Anne Bell disappears at the end of her chapter, it's only because, like Kathy Wade in O'Brien's next novel, In the *Lake of the Woods*, she enters into that permanent state of missing persons where "Mystery finally claims us all" (*In the Lake* 304).

Notes

1. Indeed, the "belated" recognition of the significance of the whole "Vietnam" experience forms a chief aspect of its conceptualization in the context of psychic trauma as I attempt to locate it here. As Cathy Caruth observes in *Unclaimed Experience*, "Traumatic experience, beyond the psychological dimension of suffering it involves, suggests a certain paradox: that the most direct seeing of a violent event may occur as an absolute inability to know it; that immediacy, paradoxically, may take the form of belatedness" (92).

2. Thus, as Tina Chen recently observed, "O'Brien's stories are not about recovering from trauma or resolving the conflicts contributing to or

created by the war in any permanent way; they are about accepting indeterminacy and learning to live not through Vietnam but with it" (80).

3. Of the three broad experiences of trauma dealt with in her important *Trauma and Recovery*, namely hysteria, shell shock, and sexual abuse (Herman 9), Judith Herman deals with the particular instance of "Vietnam" throughout her study under the second heading, and refers to O'Brien's *Things* as a leading instance (see 38, 52, 137). For similar treatments of the Vietnam experience in this psychomedical context, see also Kulka et al., Lifton, and Figley and Levantman.

4. Kali Tal references her comments specifically to Philip Beidler's *American Literature and the Experience of Vietnam* (1982), John Hellman's *American Myth and the Legacy of Vietnam* (1986), and Thomas Myers's *Walking Point: American Narratives of Vietnam* (1988), among other important theoretical works that tend to totalize the experience of the Vietnam War (Tal 218–23).

5. In Lacanian terms, the most radical restructuring of subjective "myth," as Slavoj ?i?ek points out, "triggering a traumatic crackup of our psychic balance," will come from the direction of the Real as "the previously unthinkable," hence "alien to the symbolic order" (11)—the "life substance [ironically] that proves a shock for the symbolic universe" (22). "What ultimately interrupts the continuous flow of words, what hinders the smooth running of the symbolic circuit, is the traumatic presence of the Real: when the words stay out, we have to look not for imaginary resistances but for the object that came too close" (23)—"an objectival remainder—excrement" (43). Caruth also alludes to the Lacanian address in ?i?ek to theorize trauma as "an 'escape' from the real into ideology" (*Unclaimed* 142 n. 9). ?i?ek also insightfully remarks that suicide is often at the center of subjectivity's encounter with the Real, an important aspect of O'Brien's *Things* that I shall return to later. But on the duplicitous (rather than salubrious) sense of "recovery" just scanned, ?i?ek notes that we often notice in acts of suicide "a desperate attempt to recover the traumatic encounter of the Real ... by means of integrating it into a symbolic universe of guilt, locating it within an ideological field, and thus conferring meaning upon it" (42). This last idea will gradually become clearer as we proceed.

6. On language's inability to "explicate" the trauma of war just noted, Caruth, in her important collection of essays on the subject, remarks generally upon "the way [traumatic experience] escapes full consciousness as it occurs," that it "cannot, as Georges Bataille says, become a matter of 'intelligence,'" and that "it seems to evoke the difficult truth of a history that is constituted by the very incomprehensibility of its occurrence" ("Recapturing" 153).

7. I have discussed these aspects of the Vietnam conflict at some length previously in "'Standing by His Word': The Politics of Allen

Ginsberg's Vietnam 'Vortex.'" For a further expansion of the Vietnam experience in the context of trauma as a "crisis of truth" and "a crisis of evidence," see Felman 17 and passim.

8. O'Brien's phrase here comes remarkably close to Žižek unpacking of Lacan's trauma-discourse: "even if the psychic apparatus is entirely left to itself, it will not attain the balance for which the 'pleasure principle' strives, but will continue to circulate around a traumatic intruder in its interior.... [T]he Lacanian name for this 'pleasure in pain' is of course enjoyment (*jouissance*) ... the circular movement [of] which finds satisfaction in failing again and again to attain the object" (48). For the liminal "in-betweenness of the traumatic experience, Caruth looks before Lacan to Freud, where the "temporal definition of trauma in *Beyond the Pleasure Principle* seems to be an extension of his early understanding of trauma as being locatable not in one moment alone but in the relation between two moments ... [in] the description of the traumatic experience in terms of its temporal unlocatability" (*Unclaimed* 133 n. 8).

Works by Tim O'Brien

If I Die in a Combat Zone, Box Me Up and Ship Me Home, 1973.

Northern Lights, 1975.

Going After Cacciato, 1978.

Nuclear Age, 1985.

The Things They Carried, 1990.

In the Lake of the Woods, 1994.

The Vietnam in Me, 1994.

Tomcat in Love, 1998.

July, July, 2002.

Annotated Bibliography

Scholarship on O'Brien and *The Things They Carried* is still very minimal when compared to other major literary figures. The body of work consists of very few papers (most of which are excerpted in this volume), a handful of longer interviews, and mentions in some larger scholarly works which consider writing about Vietnam in general. There are two scholarly introductions and overviews of his work, described below, but as of this writing, there has been no book-length critical work devoted solely to *The Things They Carried*.

Bates, Milton J. *The Wars We Took to Vietnam: Cultural Conflict and Storytelling*. Berkeley: University of California Press, 1996.

While considering many, many writers, the book helps to put *The Things They Carried*, as well as some of O'Brien's other work, into a cultural context. Bates illuminates the times, the several domestic issues and technological changes that made Vietnam distinctive in the American literary imagination.

Beidler, Philip D. *Re-Writing America: Vietnam Authors in Their Generation*. Athens: University of Georgia Press, 1991.

Like Bates, Beidler covers a number of authors. His main task with O'Brien is to reveal the writer's artistic forebears. Beidler claims O'Brien descends from Melville and Hemingway.

Heberle, Mark A. *Trauma Artist: Tim O'Brien and the Fiction of the Vietnam War*. Iowa City: University of Iowa Press, 2001.

Heberle considers all of O'Brien's writing through 1999 and argues the importance of "trauma" as the organizing idea of all his work.

Herzog, Toby C. *Tim O'Brien*. New York: Twayne, 1997.

Kaplan, Steven. *Understanding Tim O'Brien*. Columbia: University of South Carolina Press, 1995.

Both of the above volumes are critical introductions to O'Brien.

Naparsteck, Martin. "An Interview with Tim O'Brien." *Contemporary Literature* 32 (Spring 1991): pp. 1–11.

This is one of the longer and more illuminating of the interviews O'Brien gave close to the time of *The Things They Carried*. The only longer interview (and other one primarily focused on *The Things They Carried*, was published in the literary journal *Artful Dodge*.

Neilson, Jim. *Warring Fictions: American Literary Culture and the Vietnam War Narrative*. Jackson: University Press of Mississippi, 1998.

Neilson's book considers a wide array of literature on Vietnam, in an attempt at describing and accounting for writers' appropriating the war predominantly as an American experience. *The Things They Carried* is much discussed, particularly because Neilson is sharply critical of the book's form and the resulting celebration of it by critics.

Renny, Christopher. *The Viet Nam War, The American War*. Amherst: University of Massachusetts Press, 1995.

In a book which considers how ethnocentric attitudes have shaped the literary "canon" around the war in Viet Nam, Christopher devotes several pages to a consideration of *The Things They Carried*.

Ringnalda, Don. *Fighting and Writing the Vietnam War*. Jackson: University Press of Mississippi, 1994.

A work of literary and cultural criticism, the book features an entire chapter on O'Brien, during which Ringnalda places *The Things They Carried* in multiple contexts.

The following are the most thorough interviews of O'Brien, and the ones which deal most directly with *The Things They Carried*:

Bruckner, D.J.R. "A Storyteller for the War That Won't End." *New York Times*, (April 3, 1990): pp. C15.

Shostak, Debra. *"Artful Dodge* Interviews Tim O'Brien." *The Artful Dodge* 17 (1991):74–90.

Taylor, Mark. "Tim O'Brien's War." *The Centennial Review* 39 (Summer 1995): pp. 213–230.

 Contributors

Harold Bloom is Sterling Professor of the Humanities at Yale University. He is the author of over 20 books, including *Shelley's Mythmaking* (1959), *The Visionary Company* (1961), *Blake's Apocalypse* (1963), *Yeats* (1970), *A Map of Misreading* (1975), *Kabbalah and Criticism* (1975), *Agon: Toward a Theory of Revisionism* (1982), *The American Religion* (1992), *The Western Canon* (1994), and *Omens of Millennium: The Gnosis of Angels, Dreams, and Resurrection* (1996). *The Anxiety of Influence* (1973) sets forth Professor Bloom's provocative theory of the literary relationships between the great writers and their predecessors. His most recent books include *Shakespeare: The Invention of the Human* (1998), a 1998 National Book Award finalist, *How to Read and Why* (2000), *Genius: A Mosaic of One Hundred Exemplary Creative Minds* (2002), and *Hamlet: Poem Unlimited* (2003). In 1999, Professor Bloom received the prestigious American Academy of Arts and Letters Gold Medal for Criticism, and in 2002 he received the Catalonia International Prize.

Gabriel Welsch's short stories, poems, and reviews have appeared in *Georgia Review*, *Mid-American Review*, *Crab Orchard Review*, and *Cream City Review*. He regularly reviews literature for *Harvard Review*, *Missouri Review*, *Slope*, and *Small Press Review*. He received a Pennsylvania Council on the Arts Fellowship for Literature in fiction in 2003.

Clayton W. Lewis is a former marine officer, and a program officer for the National Endowment for the Humanities.

Pamela Smiley has taught at numerous colleges and institutions and is Chair of the English Department, and Associate Professor of English at Carthage College.

Robin Blyn is assistant professor of English and Foreign Languages at The University of West Florida.

Catherine Calloway is the director of graduate studies and Professor of English at Arkansas State University.

Maria S. Bonn has a 1990 Ph.D. from the State University of New York at Buffalo. She has taught at Sichuan international Studies university in China, Bilkent university in Turkey, and Albion College. Currently she is the Director of Scholarly Publishing at the University of michigan, University Library. She is the author of several articles on narrative and the Vietnam War, as well as more recent work on the creation of digital libraries and the development of electronic publishing.

Lorrie N. Smith teaches English and American Studies at St. Michael's College. She specializes in American poetry and African American Literature.

Steven Kaplan is President of the University of New Haven. He has taught at the University of Virginia's College at Wise, where he was Chancellor and Professor of English, and at Butler University, among others. His books include *Understanding Tim O'Brien* (1995), and *Between the Lines: International Short Stories of War* (1994) which he edited with Pauletta Otis.

Marilyn Wesley teaches English at Hartwick College. Her books include *Violent Adventure: Contemporary Fiction by American Men* (2003), *Secret Journeys: The Trope of the Woman Traveler in American Literature* (1998), *Refusal and Transgression in Joyce Carol Oates' Fiction* (1993).

David R. Jarraway has taught at Brown University, St. John's University, and the University of Ottawa. His publications include *Going the Distance Dissident Subjectivity in Modernist American Literature* (2003), and *Wallace Stevens and the Question of Belief: "Metaphysician in the Dark"* (1993).

Acknowledgments

"Chronicle of War" by Clayton Lewis. From *The Sewanee Review*, 99:2 (April–June 1991), © 1991 by the University of the South. Pp. 301–302. Reprinted with the permission of the editor.

"The Role of the Ideal (Female) Reader in Tim O'Brien's The Things They Carried: Why Should Real Women Play?" by Pamela Smiley. From *The Massachusetts Review* 43:4 (Winter 2002–2003). Pp. 602–612. Reprinted by permission from The Massachusetts Review.

"O'Brien's *The Things They Carried*" by Robin Blyn. From *The Explicator* 61:3 (Spring 2003). © 2003 by Heldref Publications. Reprinted with permission of the Helen Dwight Reid Educational Foundation.

"'How to Tell a True War Story': Metafiction in The Things They Carried" by Catherine Calloway. From *Critique* 36:4 (Summer 1995). © 1995 by Heldref Publications. Pp. 250–254. Reprinted with permission of the Helen Dwight Reid Educational Foundation.

"Can Stories Save Us? Tim O'Brien and the Efficacy of the Text" by Maria S. Bonn. From *Critique* 36:1 (Fall 1994). © 1994 by Heldref Publications. Pp. 12–15. Reprinted with permission of the Helen Dwight Reid Educational Foundation.

"'The Things Men Do': The Gendered Subtext in Tim O'Brien's Esquire Stories" by Lorrie N. Smith. From *Critique* 36:1 (Fall 1994). © 1994 by Heldref Publications. Pp. 31–38. Reprinted with permission of the Helen Dwight Reid Educational Foundation.

"The Undying Unvertainty of the Narrator in Tim O'Brien's The Things They Carried" by Steven Kaplan. From *Critique* 35:1 (Fall 1993). © 1994 by Heldref Publications. Pp. 46–52. Reprinted with permission of the Helen Dwight Reid Educational Foundation.

"Truth and Fiction in Tim O'Brien's If I Die in a Combat Zone and The Things They Carried" by Marilyn Wesley. From *College Literature* 29:2 (Spring 2002). Pp. 5–8. Reprinted by permission.

"'Excremental Assault' in Tim O'Brien: Trauma and Recovery in Vietnam War Literature" by David R. Jarraway. From *Modern Fiction Studies* 44:3 (Fall 1998). © Purdue Research Foundation. Pp. 696–701. Reprinted with permission of The Johns Hopkins University Press.

Index

Characters in literary works are indexed by first name followed by the title of the work in parentheses. Episodes (chapters) are indexed alphabetically.

143

3 1143 00732 0618